Uniforms & Equipment of the Central Powers in World War I
Volume 1

Uniforms & Equipment of the Central Powers in World War I

Volume One: Austria-Hungary & Bulgaria

- k.u.k. Kriegsmarine
- Naval Aviation
- Cavalry
- Infantry
- Artillery
- Czars and Generals
- The Kaisers

Dr. Spencer Anthony Coil

Schiffer Military History
Atglen, PA

ACKNOWLEDGMENTS

First, and foremost, I would like to acknowledge and dedicate this work to all those who served in the Great War, especially those who appear in these photographs, and above all to my family, who supported and stood by me every step of the way, especially my ***Mother***, ***Aunt Frankie***, and ***Grandmother***!

I would like to thank the following individuals who directly or indirectly assisted in the creation of this work:

Engineer / Diplom Ing. Manyo Manev from Bulgaria (historian, as well as an expert and specialist in the fields of historical documents and photos)
Patrick Gariépy
Jivko Nakev (enthusiast, expert, specialist)
Ivan Barnev (enthusiast, expert, specialist)
The Popov Family (enthusiasts, specialist)
Professor Dr. Renato Zavattini and family (experts, specialists, enthusiasts, historians, authors)
Dr. Tazio Trivini Bellini (expert, specialist, enthusiast, historian)
Enzo Bajocchi (expert, specialist, enthusiast, historian)
Frédéric Gouraud (expert, specialist, enthusiast, historian)
Steve Smith Studios (professional photographers)
Salvatore Vasta, uniform specialist, founder and curator of the Italian Front Group.
The Pomeranzeva-Halikin Family (historians, experts, enthusiasts and linguists)
The Hornkohl Family (enthusiasts)
The Otte Family (enthusiasts)
Alexei Grichine (expert, specialist and enthusiast)
Frau Dr. Grafin Irene Montjoye and her son Herr Mag. Graf Douglas Montjoye (authors, journalists, enthusiasts, historians)
Dan Eibeck (historian, expert, specialist, enthusiast, archaeologist)
Mag. Clemens Ellmauthaler (author, historian, expert, specialist, enthusiast)
Fulvio Rizzo (historian, expert, specialist, enthusiast)
Professor Del Schwinke
President Dr. David Harpool
President Dr. Wil Goodheer
Vice President Dr. L. Boyer
My Students

A special thanks to internationally acclaimed and recognized military medals and decorations experts, specialists, and enthusiasts, Herr und Frau Mag. Hartmut und Christine Rochowanski, who have maintained an impeccable reputation for over thirty years, and Franz Zabernig and family.

Finally, a very special thanks to the Schiffer team! They are all great to work with and the books just keep getting better!

Book design by Ian Robertson.

Library of Congress Control Number: 2007925907

Printed in China.
ISBN: 978-0-7643-2781-0

We are interested in hearing from authors with book ideas on related topics.

Published by Schiffer Publishing Ltd.
4880 Lower Valley Road
Atglen, PA 19310
Phone: (610) 593-1777
FAX: (610) 593-2002
E-mail: Info@schifferbooks.com.
Visit our web site at: www.schifferbooks.com
Please write for a free catalog.
This book may be purchased from the publisher.
Please include $3.95 postage.
Try your bookstore first.

In Europe, Schiffer books are distributed by:
Bushwood Books
6 Marksbury Avenue
Kew Gardens
Surrey TW9 4JF, England
Phone: 44 (0) 20 8392-8585
FAX: 44 (0) 20 8392-9876
E-mail: Info@bushwoodbooks.co.uk.
Visit our website at: www.bushwoodbooks.co.uk
Free postage in the UK. Europe: air mail at cost.
Try your bookstore first.

Contents

Introduction 6

Austria-Hungary

Chapter One: Machineguns 9
Chapter Two: General Infantry and Other Units 14
Chapter Three: Life on the Front and in the Trenches 38
Chapter Four: Medical 70
Chapter Five: Cavalry and mounted troops 82
Chapter Six: *K.u.K Kriegsmarine* / Royal and Imperial Navy 104
Chapter Seven: *K.u.K Seeflieger* / Royal and Imperial Naval Aviation 125
Chapter Eight: *Beamten* / Civil Servants 154
Chapter Nine: Pre to early war 158
Chapter Ten: Artillery 170
Chapter Eleven: Communication units 174
Chapter Twelve: The Kaisers and the Generals 178

Bulgaria

Chapter Thirteen: Machineguns 190
Chapter Fourteen: Medical 195
Chapter Fifteen: General Infantry 203
Chapter Sixteen: Life on the front and in the trenches 237
Chapter Seventeen: Artillery 285
Chapter Eighteen: Unique and unusual 296
Chapter Nineteen: Medals, Decorations and Orders 305
Chapter Twenty: Other units 313
Chapter Twenty-one: Czars and Generals 323

Color Gallery 326
Glossary 374
Further Reading 376

Introduction

Examining these photos of Austro-Hungarian *k.u.k. Soldaten* (imperial and royal soldiers) and Bulgarian *voinitzi* (soldiers) reveals how uniforms and equipment of both nations' armed forces were influenced by not only the nations of the Central Powers but by other nations before the First World War began as well. Nevertheless, Austro-Hungary and Bulgaria still maintained many traditional styles, which remained despite the foreign influence and the need to adapt to the changing demands of warfare.

Bulgaria, as well as other nations of the deteriorating Ottoman Empire, had just recently finished their courageous fight for independence during the Balkan Wars. During this period, the Bulgarian armed forces gained not only combat experience but also foreign influence from imported designs and equipment. Due to Bulgaria's geographic location, much of the influence imported was more visibly Eastern than Western in design and construction.

Austro-Hungary incorporated various uniform and equipment influences as well, due to the fact it was a multi-ethnic empire.

Headdresses

An example of both Eastern and Western influence on design and construction is visual in the Bulgarian *keppe* (field cap with visor). *Keppeta* (plural) bore a resemblance to both the Czarist Russian *furashka* (visor cap) as well as the Imperial German *Schirmmütze* (visor cap). Where *keppeta* take on more of a resemblance of *furashki* (plural) can be seen in the cockades. Both *keppeta* and *furashki* had one cockade with painted roundels that were either porcelain or an enameled metal rosette.

Like the *furashka*, the *keppe* could be given either a stiffened or crushed look. The look which was given to a *keppe* depended not always upon the individual soldier's rank but also their personal style, as was the case with the *furashka* as well (see *Uniforms and Equipment of the Czarist Russian Armed Forces*).

The Austro-Hungarian *Feldkappe* (field cap) was a distinct design way beyond its years. The design of the *Feldkappe* proved to offer a substantial amount of protection from the elements due to the fact it could cover the ear neck and throat areas (see *Uniforms and Equipment of the Austro*-Hungarian *Army in World War One* page 329). Therefore, the overall design would undergo slight modifications and remain as the field cap of Austrian and later German troops. An example is seen with the mountaineer cap (*Bergmütze*) worn by German mountain troops (*Gebirgsjäger*) during the Second World War which reflects influence from the Austro-Hungarian field cap. An interesting point to note is *Gebirgsjäger* once having received proper certification wore an Edelweiss badge (*Abzeichen*) on their *Bergmützen* (plural).

The culture and style of wearing *Kappeabzeichen* (cap badges) seemed to flourish in the Austro-Hungarian armed forces. However, other nations of the Central Powers wore *Kappeabzeichen* only on occasion.

Eastern influence is seen with the principle headdress of the *Bosniaken* (Bosnian) who wore either madder red or *feldgrau* (field gray) fez when serving in the Austro-Hungarian armed forces. Other *k.u.k. Soldaten* usually wore fezzes unofficially or as souvenirs.

Cockades of the *Feldkappe* served not only decorative and identification purposes like the Bulgarian *kokarda* but in some instances offered a means of ventilation as well.

Although the headdresses of both nations offered a distinguished appearance and substantial protection from the elements, neither was as effective as helping to prevent head injury as a steel helmet, be it either an Imperial German manufactured Model 1916 *Stahlhelm,* Austro-Hungarian *Berndorfer* or captured Model 1915 Adrian helmet.

Most of the photographs in this volume show the majority of Austro-Hungarian *Sturmtruppe* (assault troopers) and Bulgarian *Shturmovi Voyski* (assault troopers) wearing a Model 1916 German *Stahlhelm* or Bulgarian *Kaska* and in some cases a Berndorfer helmet.

Tunics

The multi-pocketed Austro-Hungarian *Feldbluse* (field tunic) remained the principal uniform cut throughout the war. Tunics could were made domestically however, many pre to mid war vintage tunics were made abroad. Due to shortages, captured Italian tunics were occasionally worn as well (see *Uniforms and Equipment of the Italian Armed Forces*).

The Bulgarians had several different models of tunics that were produced domestically or abroad. Period photos reveal *voinitzi* (soldiers) in Imperial German and Austro-Hungarian manufactured as well as Balkan War vintage tunics. Bulgarian tunics during the pre to early war years often resembled a Czarist Russian *kitel* (tunic) or a *gymnastiorka* (field blouse/tunic).

Both *k.u.k Soldaten* and *voinitzi* were seen wearing medals on their tunics in the field as well as when off active duty. It should be noted medals were made either domestically or abroad depending upon the individual soldier's access to a manufacturer.

Footwear

Footwear was a problem for all of the nations during the First World War due to material quality, shortages, and design. Bulgaria as well as other Balkan countries addressed these problems uniquely by allowing *voinitzi* to wear *opanci* or *tzarvuli*, which are a traditional style of national garb native to the Balkans. Photos of *voinitzi* wearing *opanci* or *tzarvuli* can be seen in Chapter 18.

The Austro-Hungarian armed forces also had to address the same problems with footwear. Mountaineer boots (*Bergschuhe*) worn by many locals residing in Austrian alpine regions, aided *k.u.k. Soldaten* serving in mountainous terrain. *Steigeisen* (Iron cleats used for climbing in mountainous terrain) also proved helpful.

Observations and Nuances of Both Armed Forces

As many will concur after viewing the period photographs in this volume, Bulgarian photos often show superior quality in sharpness, focus and detail over other photos taken during this period. This superior quality might be due to the individual photographer, the camera equipment or lighting conditions in the Balkans.

These photos show scenes and moments of time *k.u.k. Soldaten* or *voinitzi* wanted to share with their friends and loved ones. As stated in many of the captions following this introduction, soldiers mailed these images home as postcards, disclosing as much as they were allowed to say about their position. Some were brief others expressed themselves more. Either way, this form of correspondence allowed soldiers to send home an image with their heart felt expressions written on the reverse side.

Austria-Hungary

Chapter One

Machineguns

While the *k.u.k Soldat* (imperial and royal soldier/trooper) on the left watches for incoming enemy aircraft through his *Fernglas* (binoculars), his *Kamerad* (comrade) stands waiting to protect the aerodrome with an 8mm caliber belt-fed *Schwarzlose* mounted for anti-aircraft use. Both have rank stars and unit insignia (balloon) stitched to theirs collars.

From an elevated position three *k.u.k Soldaten* from a *Maschinengewehr Einheit* (machinegun unit) prepare to open fire on advancing enemy troops with their 8mm caliber belt-fed *Schwarzlose*. This photo is dated January 1916.

This *k.u.k Soldat* clad in *Feldgrau* (field-gray) waits for an enemy attack with his 8mm caliber belt-fed *Schwarzlose* in a sandbagged position on the frontline. 1916.

This *Maschinengewehr Einheit* dressed in *feldgrau* (field-gray) uniforms pose proudly for a group photo with their two 8mm caliber belt-fed *Schwarzlose* machineguns.

Sixteen *Soldaten* (soldiers/troops) from a *Maschinengewehr Einheit* (machinegun unit) pose for a group photo near the frontlines with their two 8mm caliber belt-fed *Schwarzlose* machineguns. Many have both rank and unit insignia stitched to the collars of their *Feldblusen* (field tunics). This photo is dated January 1918.

With two 8mm caliber belt-fed *Schwarzlose* machineguns, twelve *Soldaten* (soldiers/troops) from a *Maschinengewehr Einheit* (machinegun unit) pose proudly for a group photo. In addition to the two 8mm caliber, belt-fed *Schwarzlose* machineguns, these *Soldaten* are armed with holstered sidearms, M95 bayonets, and carbines. *Kriegs Jahr* (War Year) 1917.

Four *k.u.k Soldaten* (imperial and royal soldiers/troopers) clad in *feldgrau* (field gay) uniforms pose for a photo in the field with their 8mm caliber belt-fed *Schwarzlose* machinegun and bouquets of little flowers.

Five *k.u.k Soldaten* (imperial and royal soldiers/troopers) dressed in *feldgrau* (field gray) uniforms pause for a photo with their 8mm caliber belt-fed *Schwarzlose* machinegun before engaging incoming aircraft. On the reverse side of this photo is written "*M.G. für Fliegerabwehr bei Nowostawce*," which translates "*Machinegun used for anti-craft purposes near Nowostawce*."

Chapter Two

General Infantry and Other Units

This *k.u.k Soldat* (imperial and royal soldier/trooper) poses proudly for a photo with his canine friend in a forest clearing. He wears a *feldgrau* (field gray) wool uniform with goggles and a whistle. He is armed with an 8mm caliber Model 1895 *Steyr Mannlicher Gewehr*. The reverse side of this photo postcard is stamped "*K.k. Fußeskadron R.T.S. Feldpostamt 5.II 16.*"

The young *k.u.k Soldat* in this 1916 vintage photo postcard wears a crushable felt field cap with a cockade and cap badge. He has his Model 1912 regulation mess tin fastened to his backpack, and the strap across his chest is for his depot issued bread bag/haversack. In addition, he is armed with an 8mm caliber Model 1890 *Steyr-Mannlicher Gewehr*, bayonet, and entrenching tool.

This *k.u.k Soldat* appears ready for action as he poses for a photo armed with an 8mm caliber Model 1890 *Steyr-Mannlicher Gewehr* with fixed bayonet. This photo offers a view of his shovel with leather cover.

The two *k.u.k Soldaten* (imperial and royal soldiers/troopers) in this photo taken in Tyrol in 1917 wear uniforms made of various shades of field gray wool. The *Soldat* (soldier) on the right wears a privately purchased *Feldkappe* (field cap) made of crushable felt, while the other *Soldat* wears a depot issued *Feldkappe*. The reverse of this photo postcard is stamped *Linz 16.4.17*, and has a *Kaiserliche Königliche Österreichische Post* (Imperial Royal Austrian Post) *10 Heller* (Period Currency) *Briefmarke* (stamp) pasted on the upper right hand corner.

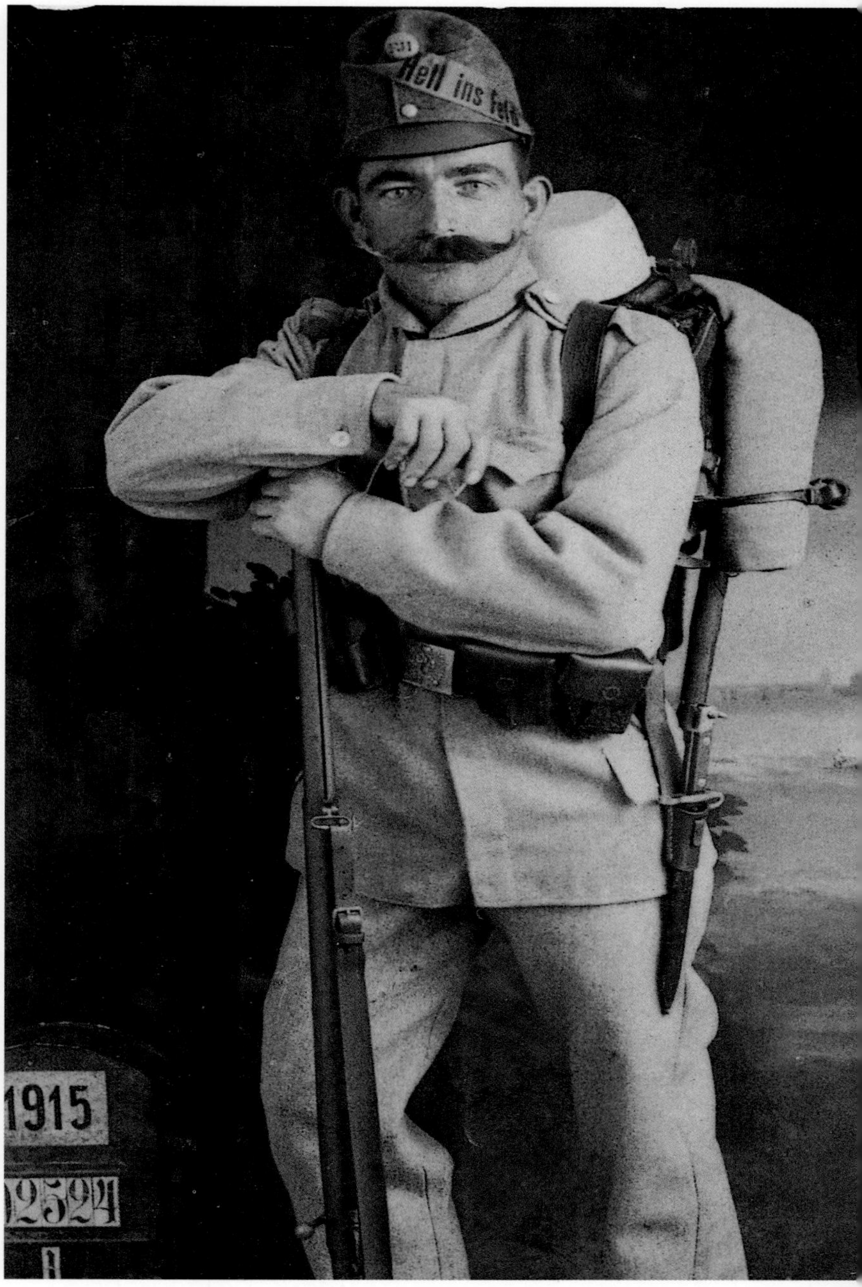

In this 1915 vintage studio photo taken in Tyrol, a *k.u.k Soldat* poses proudly dressed in his depot issued wool field uniform armed with an 8mm caliber Model 1890 *Steyr-Mannlicher Gewehr* and bayonet. His *Stiefel* (boots) are typical of those worn by pioneers. In addition, he has a Model 1899 mess kit made of tin-coated steel fastened to his backpack.

The mustached *k.u.k Soldat* in this 1915 vintage studio photo wears a *hechtgrau* (pike gray) wool field tunic and trousers with a *feldgrau* (field gray) wool field cap bearing a *FJI* (Franz Josef I) cockade, and a decorative "*Heil ins Feld*" ribbon. He is armed with an 8mm caliber bolt-action Model 1890 *Steyr-Mannlicher Gewehr*. He has a Model 1899 mess kit made of tin-coated steel fastened to his knapsack.

The *k.u.k Soldat* in this studio photo holds a brass bugle wrapped with braided cordage in his left hand, and an 8mm caliber Model 1890 *Steyr-Mannlicher Gewehr* in his right hand. His *feldgrau* (field gray) wool uniform appears to all be depot issued, and his *Stiefel* are typical of the style wore by pioneers.

This mustached soldier poses proudly for a 1917 vintage photo holding his 8mm caliber Model 1890 *Steyr-Mannlicher Gewehr* in his right hand. The strap across his chest is for his bread bag/haversack, while his shoulder straps are for his Model 1916 backpack. The roll on the tip of the right shoulder of his field tunic kept his M95 *Gewehr* from slipping off.

In this 1917 vintage photo a mustached *k.u.k Soldat* (soldier) poses for a photo clad in a *feldgrau* (field gray) wool uniform. In addition to his 8mm caliber Model 1890 *Steyr-Mannlicher* carbine with fixed bayonet, he is equipped with two Model 1895 ammo pouches and a shovel with leather carrier.

This mustached *k.u.k. Soldat* poses for a photo armed with an 8mm caliber Model 1890 *Steyr-Mannlicher Gewehr*. His field gray wool pants with braided frogging are typical for *Honvéd* (Hungarian troops/soldiers), and are referred to as *Magyarnadrág*. Flowers were often worn by new recruits, or by soldiers returning to the frontlines.

Clad in a *feldgrau* (field gray) uniform and equipped with a blanket, backpack, haversack, and pick ax, this young *k.u.k. Soldat* poses proudly for a photo armed with an 8mm caliber Model 1890 *Steyr-Mannlicher Gewehr*. On the reverse side of this photo postcard is stamped "*3./30.Marschkompagnie des I.R.47.*"

This mustached *k.u.k Soldat* wears a *hechtgrau* (pike gray) wool *Feldkappe* (field cap) *Rock* (tunic) and *Hosen* (pants). This photo displays an exceptional view of a Model 1888 ammunition pouch and a Werndl bayonet.

In this 1917 vintage photo, a mustached *k.u.k Soldat* poses wearing a *feldgrau* wool *Mantel* (overcoat) and a privately purchased crushable felt *Feldkappe* (field cap) with a FJI cockade. He is equipped with a shovel in a leather carrier, haversack, Model 1912 regulation mess tin, and a tent, which he has rolled under his backpack.

This *k.u.k. Soldat* holding his 8mm caliber Model 1890 *Steyr-Mannlicher Gewehr* in this studio photo wears a uniquely shaped *feldgrau* (field gray) wool *Feldkappe* (field cap). In addition, he is equipped with two Model 1888 leather ammunition pouches, as well as a M95 bayonet and shovel in a leather carrier.

Standing on a snow covered field, this *k.u.k Soldat* (imperial and royal soldier/trooper) poses for a photo in front of a caisson wearing a *feldgrau* (field gray) wool uniform, and armed with an 8mm caliber *Steyr-Mannlicher* carbine.

This mustached *k.u.k. Soldat* holding an 8mm caliber Model 1895 *Steyr-Mannlicher Gewehr* in his right hand poses for a late war vintage studio photo wearing a leather belt with a brass double headed eagle buckle. Fastened to his belt are mid- to late war style ammunition pouches made of sheet iron and leather. On the right side of his field cap he has fastened a Czarist Russian Officer/NCO cockade (top) and an enlisted rank cockade (bottom). In addition, he has a signal whistle hanging between his proficiency badge and his marksman cordage.

Armed with a 8mm caliber Model 1895 *Steyr-Mannlicher Gewehr* and bayonet, this *k.u.k. Soldat* poses for a photo dressed in a *hechtgrau* (pike gray) wool field cap and pair of trousers, as well as a *feldgrau* (field gray) tunic, which appears to be depot issued.

Three *k.u.k. Soldaten* clad in various shades of *hechtgrau* and *feldgrau* wool uniforms pose for a studio photo armed with 8mm caliber *Steyr-Mannlicher* carbines and fixed bayonets.

Various ranks of *k.u.k Kaiserschutzen* pose for a photo clad in issued and privately purchased field uniforms, May 1917.

Seven *k.u.k Soldaten* dressed in depot issued wool field caps, tunics, and trousers pose proudly in this magnificently clear photo postcard taken outside of their barracks. Each *Soldat* is armed with 8mm caliber bolt-action *Steyr-Mannlicher Gewehr*. A photo of one of their *Kameraden* hangs on the wall of their barracks.

Various ranks of *k.u.k Soldaten* clad in different models and cuts of field uniforms pause for a photo after a march. The reverse side of the photo postcard is stamped *17.X.15*, and pasted in the upper right corner is a *Kaiserliche Königliche Österreichische Post* (Imperial Royal Austrian Post) *5 Heller* (Period Currency) *Briefmarke* (stamp).

A group of *k.u.k. Soldaten* from various ranks pose for a photo on the side of a hill dressed in *hechtgrau* (pike gray) field tunics. Each *Soldat* is armed with an 8mm caliber bolt-action *Steyr-Mannlicher Gewehr.*

Clad in depot issued *feldgrau* (field gray) wool uniforms, forty-two *k.u.k Soldaten* pose for a late war vintage photo. Each *Soldat* is armed with an 8mm caliber bolt-action *Steyr-Mannlicher Gewehr.*

Soldaten (soldiers/troopers) from *k.u.k Infantrie Regiment 11 VI/11 Ersatz Kompanie* pose for a photo dressed in various cuts, styles, and models of uniforms, 1915.

Each armed with an 8mm caliber bolt-acton *Steyr-Mannlicher Gewehr*, this group of *k.u.k. Soldaten* pose for a photo alongside their camp tents dressed in *hechtgrau* (pike gray) wool uniforms.

K.u.k Soldaten clad in various models and cuts of field uniforms pause for a late war vintage photo in the field. Several are equipped with mid- to late war style ammunition pouches made of sheet iron and leather.

Various ranks of *k.u.k Soldaten* clad in different models and cuts of field and gala uniforms pause for a photo. Seated in the front row wearing plumed headdress is a member of the *Generalstab* (General Staff).

Nine *k.u.k. Soldaten* dressed in *hechtgrau* (pike gray) wool tunics and trousers and *dunkel blau* (dark blue) wool field caps pose for a photo in a forest clearing. Each *Soldat* is armed with an 8mm caliber bolt-action *Steyr-Mannlicher Gewehr*, and equipped with an early model leather ammunition/general purpose pouch.

A group of *k.u.k Soldaten* clad in various models of uniforms made from different materials. Many of these *Soldaten* are armed with an 8mm caliber bolt-action *Steyr-Mannlicher Gewehr*.

K.u.k Soldaten armed with 8mm caliber bolt-action *Steyr-Mannlicher* carbines.

In their barracks courtyard, *k.u.k Soldaten* clad in various models of uniforms line up for a 1917 vintage photo postcard. Each *Soldat* is armed with an 8mm caliber bolt-action *Steyr-Mannlicher Gewehr*. The reverse of this photo postcard is stamped *6.V.17*, and pasted in the upper right corner is a *Kaiserliche Königliche Österreichische Post* (Imperial Royal Austrian Post) *10 Heller* (Period Currency) *Briefmarke* (stamp).

Twelve *k.u.k Soldaten* dressed in depot issued *feldgrau* (field gray) uniforms pose for a photo during *Weihnachten* (Christmas).

The *edelweiss* collar insignia on this soldier's uniform was a style preferred by *Kaiserschützen*. In addition, he has a signal whistle hanging between his proficiency badge and his marksman *Schnur* (aiguillette/cordage).

Two *Kameraden* (comrades) pose for a mid- to late war vintage photo postcard wearing depot issued uniforms. The lanyards around their necks attach to their holstered Model 1898 Rast and Gasser revolvers. This photo offers an excellent display of the clip used to attach the lanyard to the ring on the revolver. The clips were made of metal, and had to be pressed hard to remove. This way the clip would not just fall off.

This mustached *k.u.k Soldat* poses for a photo dressed in a privately purchased *feldgrau* (field gray) field uniform while resting peacefully at the base of a statue of the Blessed Virgin.

Three *k.u.k Soldaten* pose for a studio photo clad in various shades of *feldgrau* (field gray) wool field uniforms. The mustached *Soldat* seated in the center is armed with a Werndl bayonet, while the other two *Soldaten* are armed with M1895 bayonets.

The four *k.u.k. Soldaten* in this oval shaped studio photo wear *feldgrau* (field gray) wool field tunics, trousers, and caps. Three of the *Soldaten* wear depot issued field caps, while the other wears a coarse wool knit cap.

The *k.u.k. Soldat* posing with his female companion in this late war vintage studio photo wears a uniform made of *ersatz* material.

Posing with his female companion, the dark haired and mustached *k.u.k. Soldat* in this studio photo wears a *feldgrau* (field gray) tunic with rank stars on the collar. He has a signal whistle hanging between his proficiency badge and his *Schnur* (aiguillette/cordage).

Three decorated Austro-Hungarian officers and a decorated German officer pose for a late war vintage photo. Photos such as this one reflect a strong sentiment of *Waffenbrüder*, or Brothers in Arms.

An Austro-Hungarian *Soldat* dressed in a *hechtgrau* (pike gray) uniform and an Imperial German *Soldat* dressed in *feldgrau* (field gray) pose for a studio photo. Photos such as this one reflect a strong sentiment of *Waffenbrüder*, or Brothers in Arms.

Austro-Hungarian and Imperial German *Soldaten* (soldiers/troopers) from a *Grenzkontrolle* (Border Control) unit pose for a photo dressed in various shades and models of *feldgrau* (field gray) wool uniforms.

Fourteen Austro-Hungarian and Imperial German *Soldaten* (soldiers/troopers) pause for a photo in their frontline position.

Chapter Three

Life on the Front and in the Trenches

Two *k.u.k Soldaten* (imperial and royal soldiers/troopers) prepare to engage an enemy from a rocky position.

K.u.k. Soldaten dressed in *feldgrau* (field gray) wool uniforms and equipped with gasmasks and haversacks kneel in prayer during a *Feldmesse*, or Field Mass.

This is a commercially produced photo postcard "*Das erste Gebet für Kaiser und König Karl*," or "The First Prayer for Emperor and King Karl," *24.11.1916*.

This is a commercially produced photo postcard depicting *k.u.k. Soldaten* renewing or retaking their oaths during a *Feldmesse* (Field Mass), *24.11.1916*.

This is a commercially produced photo postcard depicting *k.u.k. Soldaten* dressed in *feldgrau* (field gray) wool uniforms renewing or retaking their oaths during a *Feldmesse* (Field Mass), *24.11.1916*.

K.u.k. *Soldaten* dressed in *feldgrau* (field gray) wool uniforms and armed with M1895 bayonets kneel in prayer during a *Feldmesse* (Field Mass).

Pioneers constructing a pontoon bridge, 1916.

Clad in their battle gear, this group of *k.u.k. Soldaten* prepare to advance on an enemy position.

K.u.k. Soldaten clad in a variety of uniforms pause for a commemorative photo while building a shelter.

K.u.k. Soldaten dressed in *feldgrau* (field gray) wool uniforms pause for a late war vintage photo at their observation post.

Dressed in *feldgrau* (field gray) wool field tunics with *edelweiss* collar insignia, and armed with an 8mm caliber bolt-action *Steyr-Mannlicher* carbines, two *k.u.k Soldaten* pose for a photo at their post near the frontlines.

Various ranks of *k.u.k Soldaten* dressed in a variety of *hechtgrau* (pike gray) wool uniforms pose for a group photo at the base of a mountain.

K.u.k *Soldaten* observing well fed pigs. This photo is dated 1916.

K.u.k. Soldaten dressed in depot issued *feldgrau* (field gray) wool field uniforms pose for a 1917 vintage group photo. The boots the *Soldaten* in the front row have on are a typical style for those who served in pioneer units.

A group of *k.u.k Soldaten* clad in *hechtgrau* (pike gray) wool uniforms pose for a early to mid-war vintage photo. Each is armed with either an 8mm caliber bolt action *Steyr-Mannlicher Gewehr* or carbine. The reverse of this photo postcard is stamped "*Zensuriet*" (Censored), "*Von der Armee im Felde*" (From the army in the field), and "*K.k. Landwehr Ersatz-Bataillon Nr. 10 Proviantur.*"

K.u.k Soldaten from various ranks, and dressed in a variety of uniforms aboard a boat on the *Donau* (Danube).

Seven *Sibirisches* (Siberian) *Wiener* (Viennese) dressed in depot issued *feldgrau* (field gray) wool field uniforms pose for a photo outside their log cabin in Siberia.

K.u.k. *Soldaten* dressed in *feldgrau* (field gray) wool field uniforms pose for a photo outside of a cottage in the countryside with two Czarist Russian *frontoviki* (Russian for frontline troops) wearing *furashki* (visor caps), and holding their *shineli* (heavy wool overcoats).

Various ranks of k.u.k *Soldaten* dressed in a variety of *feldgrau* (field gray) wool uniforms pose for a group photo with their *Kameraden* (Comrades). The officer in the center wears a black wool *Ausgang Kepi* (walking out cap), which was a popular style during the war.

A group of *k.u.k Soldaten* dressed in *feldgrau* (field gray) wool and brown corduroy uniforms bivouac in a forest near the frontlines. Several have been awarded bravery medals, and have metal cap badges bearing various wartime motifs fastened to their *Schiffchen* (forage caps). The mustached *Soldat* standing on the right appears to be calling in or receiving orders on a field telephone.

Various ranks of *k.u.k Soldaten* dressed in a variety of *hechtgrau* (pike gray) wool uniforms pose for a group photo. All but the officer in the center with a saber at his side are armed with 8mm caliber bolt-action *Steyr Mannlicher* rifles.

Above: This photo postcard offers a view of an Austro-Hungarian position near mountainous terrain, 1916. Below: Twelve *k.u.k Soldaten* dressed in a variety of *feldgrau* (field gray) wool uniforms pose for a group photo. Many are armed with bolt-action rifles, and have tin coated steel Model 1899 mess kits fastened to their knapsacks.

A group of *k.u.k. Soldaten* clad in a variety of *feldgrau* (field gray) wool uniforms pose for a group photo. Many are armed with 8 mm caliber bolt-action *Steyr-Mannlicher Stutzen*, and equipped with haversacks and aluminum Model 1909 canteens. The soldier second from the end on the right wears a madder red wool fez, and is most likely a *Bosniak* (Bosnian).

Nineteen *k.u.k. Soldaten* dressed in depot issued wool field uniforms pose for a group photo. Each is armed with an 8mm bolt-action *Steyr-Mannlicher Gewehr*, 17 April 1916.

Above: A rugged looking group of pioneers pose for a group photo clad in a variety of depot issued uniforms. Many are armed with either an 8mm bolt-action *Steyr-Mannlicher Stutzen* or a saber, which had either wood or bone grips on the handle. Below: Three *k.u.k Soldaten* enjoy a meal from their tin coated Model 1912 mess kit inside their quarters on the front. All three appear to be wearing depot issued *feldgrau* (field gray) wool tunics. Each has been awarded the Kaiser Karl *Truppen Kreuz* medal. This photo was most likely taken during the Christmas season, judging by the photos of loved ones and the decoration on the table. The reverse side of this photo postcard is stamped "*Infanteriegeschützabteilung k.u.k. Infanterieregiment.*"

Ten *k.u.k. Soldaten* clad in *feldgrau* (field gray) uniforms, and a Czarist Russian soldier wearing a *furashka* (visor cap) and *shinel* (heavy wool overcoat) from the *Sibirische Mènage* (Siberian Establishment/Household) pose for a photo outside the login cabin barracks.

Weihnachten 1916, Sibirien. Christmas 1916 in Siberia.

This *Feld Postkarte* (field postcard) was sent by a *k.u.k Soldat* to his mother while he was in a *Versorgungsheim* (Care Home) in Linz. He writes that he hopes she can find him in this picture he has sent of his *Kompanie*. He asks how the others are doing back home, and he closes by writing his mother that he sends her his fondest heartfelt greetings and all his love. This *Feld Postkarte* is dated *Im Felde vom 24. März 1917* (In the Field from March 24, 1917) and *Aufnahme vom 28. März 1917* (Photo taken on March 28, 1917).

K.u.k. Soldaten clad in *feldgrau* (field gray) uniforms partake in target practice in a village near the frontlines, 1917.

Above: *K.u.k. Soldaten* dressed in *feldgrau* (field gray) uniforms pose with their canine companions in this 1917 vintage photo. *Hundetraingespann* (Dog Transport Teams) were used effectively by the armed forces during the First World War. This photo offers a detailed view of the dog's harness. Below: *Hundetraingespann* (Dog Transport Teams) pause for a photo by a cottage near the frontlines, 1917.

Above: Eleven *k.u.k. Soldaten* dressed in *feldgrau* (field gray) uniforms pose for a photo in a snowy wood. Some of these *Soldaten* are armed with holstered Model 1898 Rast and Gasser revolvers. Below: Five *K.u.k. Soldaten* dressed in *feldgrau* (field gray) uniforms outside of their snow covered mountain outpost in the Dolomite mountains.

Twenty-two *K.u.k. Soldaten* wearing depot issued *feldgrau* (field gray) uniforms pose for a photo at the edge of a snow dusted forest. Their tunics are based on the Model 1916, and some of these *Soldaten* are armed with holstered Model 1898 Rast and Gasser revolvers.

Eight *K.u.k. Soldaten* dressed in depot issued *feldgrau* (field gray) uniforms pose for a 1916 vintage in a rock covered field. Each is armed with an 8mm caliber bolt-action *Steyr Mannlicher Stutzen*.

Two *k.u.k. Soldaten* clad in depot issued *feldgrau* (field gray) uniforms pose for a photo at the entrance of their dugout on the frontline. The *Soldat* on the left, with a pair of binoculars (*Fernglas*) hanging from a leather strap, wears an Austro-Hungarian manufactured *Berndorfer* steel helmet.

Fourteen *k.u.k. Soldaten* dressed in depot issued *feldgrau* (field gray) uniforms pose for a photo outside the log cabin outpost. *Weihnachten* (Christmas) 1916.

Seven *k.u.k. Soldaten* clad in depot issued *feldgrau* (field gray) uniforms pose for a photo with their *Christ/Weihnachtsbaum* (Christmas tree). *Weihnachten* (Christmas) 1917.

Clad in well worn depot issued *feldgrau* (field gray) uniforms, and armed with holstered sidearms, nine *k.u.k. Soldaten* pose proudly with 8mm caliber belt-fed *Schwarzlose*. Three of these *Soldaten* wear Austro-Hungarian manufactured *Berndorfer* steel helmets.

K.u.k. Soldaten dressed in depot issued *feldgrau* (field gray) uniforms pause for a photo while waiting patiently in their trenches for an enemy advance.

Four relaxing *k.u.k. Soldaten* wearing *feldgrau* (field gray) uniforms pose for a photo with their canine companions.

A decorated group of *k.u.k Soldaten* wearing overcoats (*Mantel*) poses proudly for a late war vintage photo. Each wears either a Model 1916 *Stahlhelm* or a *Berndorfer*.

K.u.k. Soldaten clad in *feldgrau* (field gray) uniforms pose for a photo with their canine companion in the snow. The *k.u.k Soldat* on the right has cap badges fastened to his *Schiffchen* (forage cap).

Three *k.u.k. Soldaten* dressed in *feldgrau* (field gray) tunics and trousers pose for a photo outside of their bunker on the frontlines. Each wears an Austro- Hungarian manufactured *Berndorfer* steel helmet.

Nine *k.u.k. Soldaten* clad in *feldgrau* (field gray) uniforms pose for a late war vintage photo with artillery projectiles/rounds resting on their table.

This *k.u.k Soldat* poses for a photo at his position on the frontline wearing an Austro-Hungarian manufactured *Berndorfer* steel helmet and a *feldgrau* (field gray) wool overcoat (*Mantel*). In addition, he is equipped with *Handgranaten* (hand grenades).

In a wooded area near the frontlines, five *k.u.k. Soldaten* dressed in *feldgrau* (field gray) uniforms pause for a photo before enjoying a meal.

Wearing a Model 1916 *Stahlhelm* and a *feldgrau* (field gray) wool tunic (*Rock/Bluse*), this *k.u.k Soldat* poses for a photo equipped with *Handgranaten* (hand grenades) and an Austro-Hungarian manufactured gasmask.

K.u.k Soldaten driving up a mountain road, 1916.

Parked on a dirt road, a group of *k.u.k Soldaten* (imperial and royal soldiers/troopers) pause for a photo with their vehicle before continuing their drive.

K.u.k Soldaten in a snowy wood pause for a photo in a horse drawn sleigh, 1916.

In a snow covered field near the frontlines, two *K.u.k Soldaten* pause for a photo in their horse drawn sleigh. The driver holding the reins wears a *feldgrau* (field gray) wool *Schiffchen* (forage cap), and the mustached officer riding with him wears a privately purchased *feldgrau Kepi*.

Above: Mustached and bearded *k.u.k. Soldaten* dressed in *feldgrau* (field gray) uniforms pose for a photo. Several have a pair of snow goggles (*Schnee Brille*), and two have binoculars (*Fernglas*), Lusia, 1916. Below: *K.u.k. Soldaten* clad in a variety of uniforms pose for a photo equipped with various models of gasmasks.

K.u.k. Soldaten dressed in *feldgrau* (field gray) uniforms pause for a photo while bravely awaiting an enemy attack on their position.

Two *k.u.k. Soldaten* dressed in *feldgrau* (field gray) uniforms pose for a photo outside their tent while enjoying a drink. This photo offers a detailed view of the tent fittings.

Courageously awaiting an enemy attack on their snow cover position, *k.u.k. Soldaten* dressed in *feldgrau* (field gray) uniforms pose for a photo armed with 8mm bolt action Model 1895 *Steyr Mannlicher* rifles. The mustached *Soldat* wearing a *feldgrau* (field gray) wool *Mantel* (overcoat) and *Feldkappe* (field cap) is armed with an M95 *Gewehr* with fixed bayonet and *Rohr* hand grenade.

Ukrainian Legionnaire and patriot Olena Stepanivna was appointed commander of a rifle platoon, and fought in combat against the Russians. She earned the *Silbernes Tapferkeitsmedaille* (Silver Bravery Medal), and was a graduate of the University of Lviv.

Chapter Four

Medical

Two nuns/sisters pose with eight *k.u.k Soldaten* in a military hospital. Nuns worked often as *Krankenschwester* (Nurses) in military hospitals throughout the First World War.

A mustached medic with three medals stitched to his tunic poses proudly for a photo with fifteen volunteer nurses.

K.u.k Soldaten and hospital staff pose for a late war vintage photo. The sign reads "*k.u.k Kriegsspital St. Pölten Küche.*" (Royal and Imperial War/Veterans Hospital St. Pölten Kitchen).

Three medics dressed in *feldgrau* (field gray) uniforms pose for a photo with two nurses. The mustached medic in the center wears a *Rotes Kreuz* (Red Cross) badge. Although a larger size, his badge has the same motif as the badge featured in the color gallery on page 326 column 4 in *Uniforms and Equipment of the Austro-Hungarian Army in World War One*.

Nurses pose with their patients in this mid- to late war vintage photo, Kaisermühlen 1915.

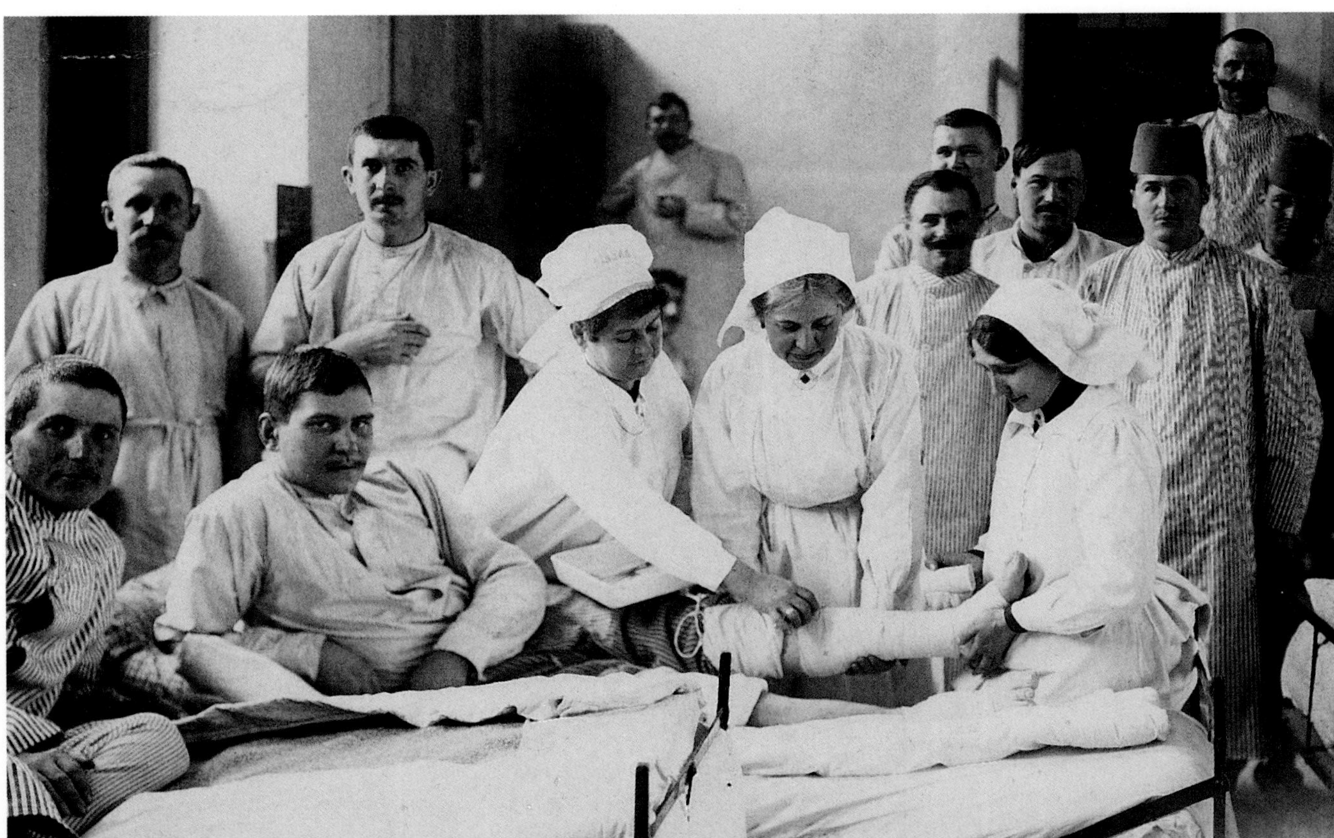

K.u.k Soldaten pose for a photo in a military hospital while the nurses tend to a bandage on their *Kamerad* (comrade). Written on the reverse side of this photo postcard is *Kriegsjahr* (War Year) 1914-15.

Two nurses pose for a studio photo with three *k.u.k Soldaten* clad in depot issued *feldgrau* (field gray) wool uniforms and holding canes. *Kriegsjahr* (War Year) 1914-15.

Outside of the *2 Chirurgie Abteilung* (2nd Surgery Detachment), two nurses pose for a photo with *k.u.k Soldaten* clad in depot issued uniforms made from various shades of *feldgrau* (field gray) wool.

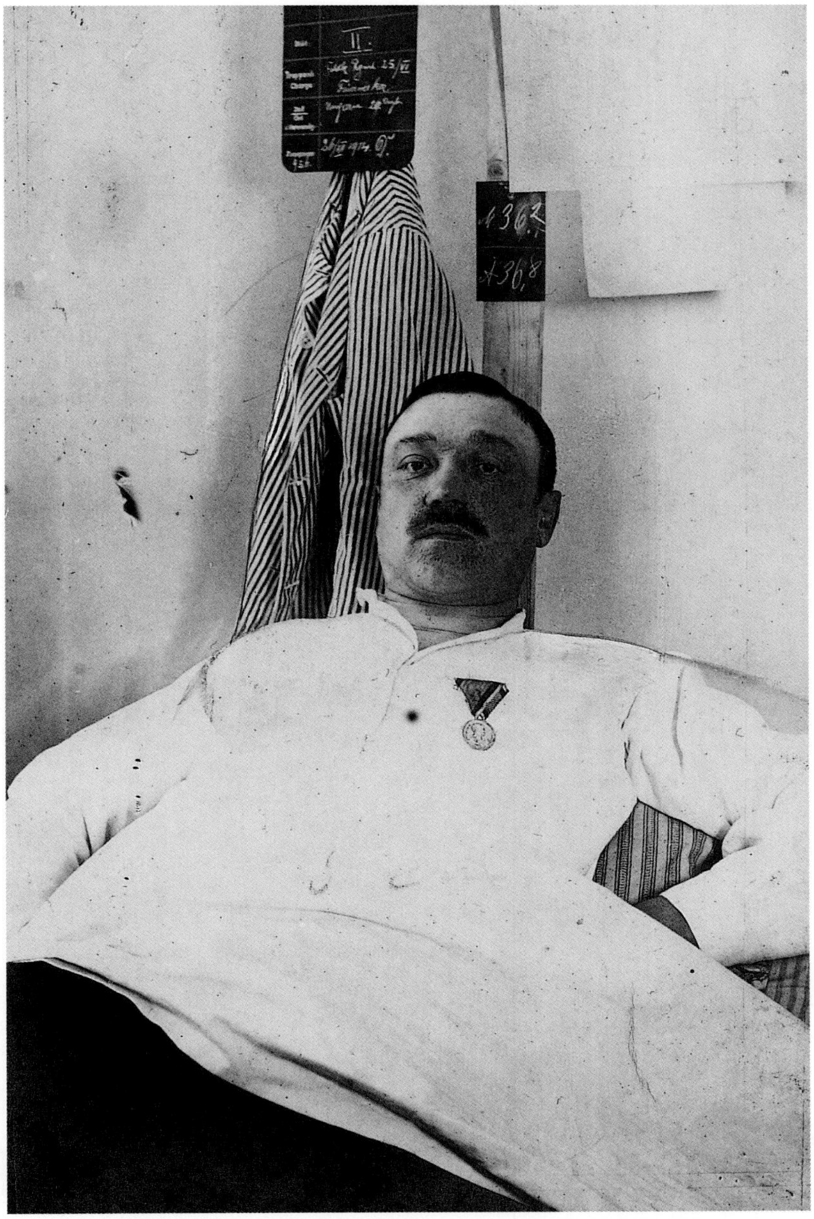

This *k.u.k Soldat* poses proudly for a photo wearing his *Tapferkeit Medaillen/Orden* (Bravery Medal).

Two nurses and twenty-one *k.u.k. Soldaten* dressed in various models of uniforms pose for a photo in a military hospital. Seated in front of the nurse wearing a black bonnet is a *Zugsführer* decorated with bravery and other medals.

K.u.k Kriegsspital (Royal and Imperial War/Veterans Hospital), 1915.

Nurses, surgeons, and *k.u.k Soldaten* pose for a late war vintage photo inside their barracks.

Nurses, surgeons, and *k.u.k Soldaten* pose for a late war vintage photo inside a military hospital.

K.u.k Soldaten pause from their daily activities at a *k.u.k Kriegsspital* (Royal and Imperial War/Veterans Hospital) for a late war vintage photo.

Three *k.u.k Soldaten* pose for a photo dressed in their nightshirts. *Fröhliche Weihnachten im Kriegs-Jahr 1914* (Merry Christmas in the year of the war 1914).

A nurse poses with her patients outside of a military hospital for a late war vintage photo.

Above: Three *k.u.k Soldaten* clad in depot issued *feldgrau* (field gray) wool uniforms pose for a photo with their vehicle, which bears medical unit insignia. Below: Surgery procedures during the First World War.

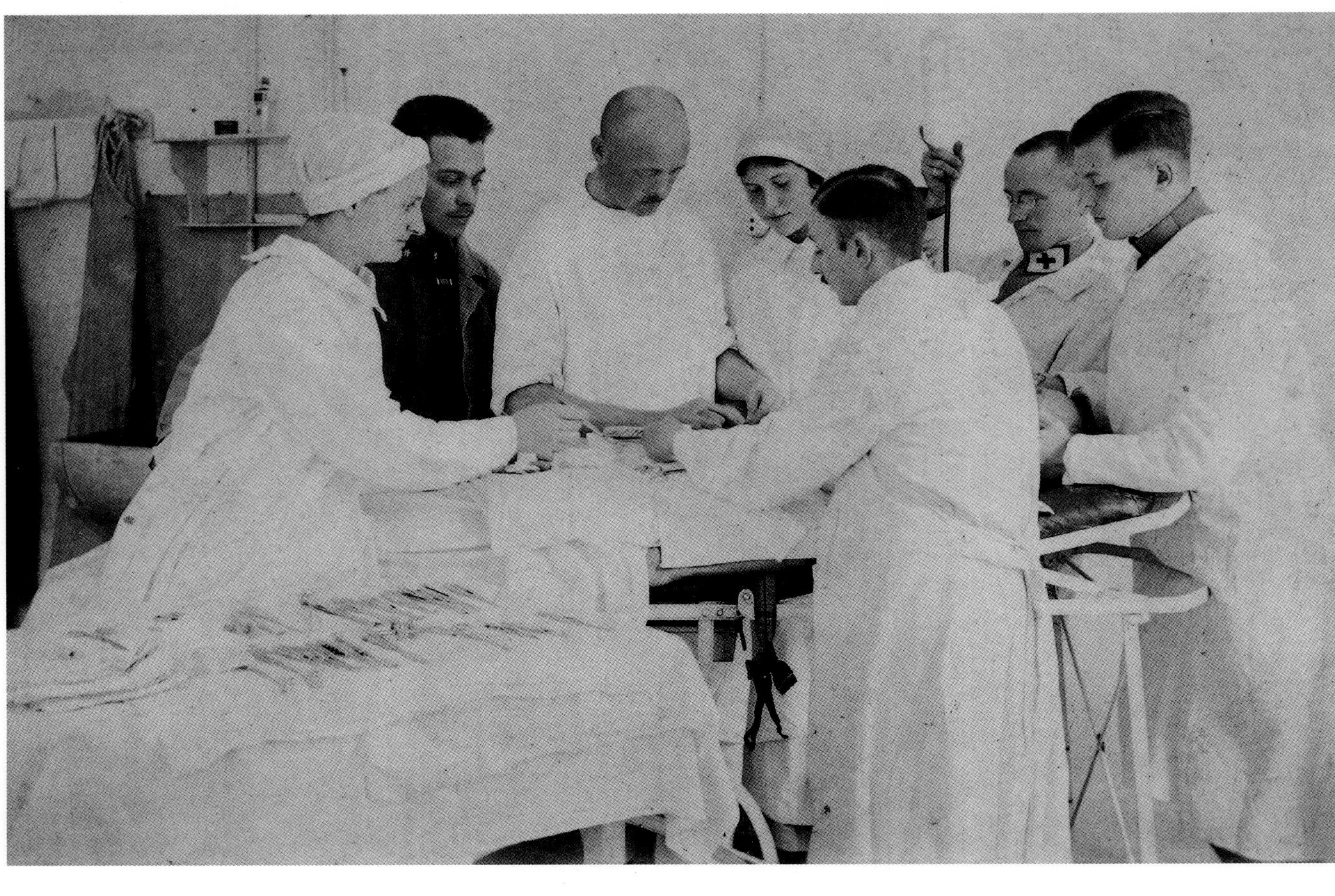

This mustached *Sanitäter* (medic) wearing a *feldgrau* (field gray) wool tunic and pair of trousers poses for a studio photo with his female companion. In addition, he has a *3 Armee* (3rd Army) badge fastened above the cordage on his tunic.

The *Sanitäter* (medic) clutching his saber in this studio photo wears a *feldgrau* (field gray) wool field cap, tunic, and trousers. In addition, he has a *Rot Kreuz* (Red Cross) badge pinned above his left breast pocket.

Chapter Five

Cavalry and Mounted Troops

A pre- to early war photo of Hussars enjoying food and drink. One Hussar wears his Shako, and the others wear their black wool *Ausgang Kepis* (walking-out caps/kepis). Several of these Hussars wear a style of tunic known as an/the Attila.

The mustached Hussar in this pre- to early war cabinet portrait wears a style of wool tunic known as an Attila with *die Jubiläums-Medaillen 1898* (1898 Crown Jubilee Medal).

The Hussar resting his right arm on a chair in this pre- to early war cabinet portrait is dressed in a style of wool tunic known as an Attila.

Posing with his female companion in this pre- to early war cabinet portrait is a mustached Hussar dressed in a wool tunic known as an Attila. The intricate gold stitching on the cuffs of his tunic was a style that would have been preferred by a *Magyar* (Hungarian) *Huszár* (Hussar). He has several decorations stitched to his Attila, as well.

In this pre- to early war cabinet portrait, a mustached Hussar clad in an Attila poses proudly with his female companion. This photo was taken in Klagenfurt.

The mustached Hussar in this pre- to early war cabinet portrait taken in *Ungarische* (Hungarian) Weisskirchen wears a style of wool tunic known as an Attila.

This mustached Ulan dressed in a ten button tunic poses proudly with his lovely wife and daughter in this pre- to early war cabinet portrait. He is decorated with *die Jubiläums-Medaillen 1898* (1898 Crown Jubilee Medal) as well.

This Ulan dressed in a fur lined double-breasted wool jacket (*Ulanka*) poses proudly for a pre- to early war studio photo with his wife and children.

With his saber with sword knot tucked under his left arm, this mustached Ulan poses proudly for a pre- to early war studio photo wearing a privately tailored tunic and a cavalry helmet for lancers (*Tshapka*). In addition, he is armed with a holstered Model 1898 Rast and Gasser revolver and Model 1898 leather ammunition pouch.

Gazing at his female companion, the mustached Ulan in this pre- to early war vintage cabinet portrait wears a black wool *Ausgang Kepi* (walking out cap/kepi) and a privately tailored ten button tunic. He has been decorated with *die Jubiläums-Medaillen 1898* (1898 Crown Jubilee Medal), and is armed with a saber with sword knot.

The Dragoon in this pre- to early war vintage cabinet portrait poses proudly wearing a six-button tunic and a fur lined jacket. He is armed with a saber.

The mounted Dragoon in this early war vintage photo wears a *Dragoneroffiziershelm M. 1850* (Dragoon officer's helmet Model 1850), and is equipped with riding and combat gear.

This group of Dragoons is equipped with signal and observation equipment.

Dragoons and *k.u.k Soldaten* from other branches of the armed forces. This photo postcard was sent to Wiener Neudorf, as the writing on the reverse side indicates. There is also a date and location written (Brunn, *8.14.1913*).

Nine Dragoons armed with sabers enjoying a drink. Many of these Dragoons have earned proficiency badges as well.

Five Dragoons wearing madder red forage caps and wool tunics with sulfur yellow collars and cuffs pose for a photo outside their barracks.

This Dragoon, wearing a madder red *Schiffchen* (forage cap) and armed with a saber, poses for a photo with a friend on a muddy road. In addition, this Dragoon has been awarded two proficiency badges, which he has fastened to his tunic.

This mustached Dragoon wearing a madder red *Schiffchen* (forage cap), and armed with a saber, poses proudly for a photo mounted on his horse.

This *k.u.k Soldat* dressed in a depot issued *hechtgrau* (pike gray) wool uniform, and equipped with a haversack/bread bag and leather Model 1888 ammunition pouches, poses for a photo with his horse before riding off to battle.

Two mustached *k.u.k Soldaten* dressed in depot issued *feldgrau* (field gray) wool uniforms pose proudly for a photo with their horse. Both *Soldaten* are armed with sabers and holstered side arms.

K.u.k Soldaten pose proudly with two well groomed white horses.

Two *k.u.k Soldaten* dressed in summer weight uniforms pose for a photo with their horse and sleeping canine companion. The mounted *k.u.k Soldat* wears a black wool *Ausgang Kepi* (walking out cap-kepi), and the other *Soldat* holding the reins wears a depot issued *Feldkappe* (field cap).

This mounted *k.u.k Soldat* wears a privately purchased crushable felt field cap and tunic with trousers. He is equipped with leather saddlebags, and is armed with a holstered side arm.

On a dirt road enroute to the frontlines, two *k.u.k Soldaten* wearing forage caps pose proudly for a photo with their horses.

Wearing a privately tailored *feldgrau* (field gray) uniform, this *k.u.k Soldat* poses for a photo with his neatly groomed horse. He is armed with a saber, and equipped with a unique style of saddlebag.

In this 1915 vintage photo, three *k.u.k Soldaten* dressed in *feldgrau* (field gray) wool uniforms pose for a photo with their horses before riding off to the frontlines.

Mounted on his white horse, this *k.u.k Soldat* poses proudly for a photo dressed in a *feldgrau* (field gray) wool uniform and armed with a saber.

This *k.u.k Soldat* poses proudly for a photo while mounted on his horse. He has a Model 1899 tin-coated mess tin fastened to his bedroll, and he has an enamel canteen with leather carrying straps.

Above: Armed with a saber, this *k.u.k. Soldat* poses proudly for a photo while mounted on his horse. Below: A pre- to early war photo post depicting mounted *k.u.k. Soldaten*.

Wearing a well worn depot issued *feldgrau* (field gray) wool uniform, this mustached *k.u.k. Soldat* poses proudly for a photo holding the reins of his white horse. This photo postcard offers an exceptional view of the saddle.

Before riding further on a dirt road enroute to the frontlines, this mustached *k.u.k. Soldat* poses for a photo while holding the reins of his horse. He is equipped with a Model 1895 bayonet, as well as with a gasmask in a canister.

Armed with a saber and equipped with saddle bags, this *k.u.k. Soldat* pauses for a photo with his horse before continuing to battle.

With his decorations fastened proudly to his *feldgrau* (field gray) *Karl's Bluse* (tunic), this mustached *k.u.k Soldat* poses for a photo on his horse near a stone wall. He is equipped with a Model 1895 bayonet and saddlebags.

This *k.u.k Soldat* dressed in a privately tailored *feldgrau* (field gray) wool uniform poses for a photo while mounted on his white horse. He is equipped with saddlebags, a dispatch case, and a Model 1899 tin-coated mess tin with cloth cover fastened to his bed roll.

In this pre- to early war vintage photo a *k.u.k. Soldat* armed with a saber poses proudly on his massive horse.

With his saber drawn, an Ulan wearing a *Ulanka* and *Tshapka* addresses a high ranking Hussar dressed in an Attila. Kaiser Karl, when visiting the front or troops on maneuvers, often wore this style of an Attila.

Chapter Six

K.u.k Kriegsmarine (Imperial and Royal Navy)

The U28 on the Adriatic. The U28 was manufactured in Pola/Pula.

Above: The U1 "Lake" class/type in training on the Adriatic. Below: The U12 on the Adriatic. In December 1914 the U12 was damaged by a French dreadnought and was lost in August 1915 in Venice Lagoon with all crew on board.

The U12 was a "Holland" class/type U-Boot /Submarine.

The U14 was formerly the French "*Curie*" until entering Austro-Hungarian service. The U14 was sunk in December 1914, and later raised January 1915. In October 1915 it was placed under the command of *Ritter* (Knight/ Sir) Georg von Trapp.

Built in Kiel, Germany, the U17 was launched in February 1915, and entered service in June 1915.

The U4 was launched in November 1908, and entered service in August 1909. The U4 had twenty-one crewmembers, and was manufactured in Kiel, Germany.

The U1 on the waters of the Adriatic.

The U1 preparing to dive.

Heavy artillery on the *S.M.S Tegetthoff*.

Küstentorpedoboot II/02 (Coastal Torpedo Boat II/02) on the Adriatic.

K.u.k *Matrosen* (Imperial and royal sailors/seamen) dressed in their navy whites with dark blue wool caps pause for a photo before loading a torpedo.

Inspecting the torpedo chamber aboard the *S.M.S. Prinz Eugen.*

Above: The torpedo room of the *S.M.S. Prinz Eugen*. Below: Pola, 1915.

The S.M.S. *Radetsky* on the Adriatic.

K.u.k Matrosen aboard the *S.M.S. Tegetthoff.*

The *Turul* and crew on the waters of the Adriatic.

S.M.S. *Tegetthoff* anchored in the Adriatic.

S.M.S. *Habsburg* at dock.

Küstentorpedoboot 04/IV (Coastal Torpedo Boat 04/IV) on the Adriatic.

K.u.k *Matrosen* (Imperial and royal sailors/seamen) clad in various uniforms aboard the *S.M.S Prinz Eugen*.

K.u.k *Matrosen* (Imperial and royal sailors/seamen) resting on the deck of the *S.M.S. Habsburg*.

K.u.k *Matrosen* (Imperial and royal sailors/seamen) exercising aboard the S.M.S. *Habsburg*. Each *Matrose* (sailor/seamen) holds a training rifle (*Übungsgewehr*) made of wooc with metal fittings.

Clad in sullied white naval fatigues, this mustached *k.u.k. Matrose* (Imperial and royal sailors/seamen) prepare to load a round into the chamber of an artillery piece aboard the *S.M.S Prinz Eugen*.

K.u.k Matrosen (Imperial and royal sailors/seamen) of the *S.M.S Prinz Eugen* loading a torpedo.

Three *k.u.k Matrosen* of the *S.M.S. Szent Istvan* pose for a photo wearing two styles of underwater breathing devices.

Weihnachten (Christmas) aboard the *S.M.S. Reka*, 1915.

An officer in his quarters aboard the *S.M.S. Habsburg*.

Above: *K.u.k Matrosen* (Imperial and royal sailors/seamen) clad in dark blue wool uniforms on the deck of the *S.M.S. Habsburg*. Below: Aboard the *S.M.S. Habsburg*, *k.u.k Matrosen* (Imperial and royal sailors/seamen) parade past naval bandsmen.

The U18 on the Adriatic.

K.u.k. Matrosen preparing their assault/battle gear on the deck of an *Erherzogklasse Schalcht Schiff* (Archduke Class Battleship).

Hooded *k.u.k Matrosen* prepare to fire an artillery piece known as a *Schnellfeuerkanone*.

K.u.k. Matrosen clad in dark navy blue wool and white cotton uniforms pose for a photo aboard the *S.M.S Erzherzog Ferdinand Max*.

19cm caliber artillery piece aboard the *S.M.S. St. Georg*.

The crew of the *E.H.Albrecht*.

K.u.k. Matrosen dressed in sullied navy fatigues pose for a photo with their *Schiff* (Ship) while clinging to the moorings and anchors.

The S.M.S. *Radetzky* anchored.

In this cabinet portrait dated *3.1.1914*, a *k.u.k. Matrose* poses proudly dressed in his dark blue wool navy uniform, and armed with a Model 1895 bayonet. The tally on his cap indicates he is from the *S.M.S. Radetzky*.

Chapter Seven

Seeflieger (Naval Aviation)

Three mustached naval aviators (*Seeflieger/piloten*) pose for a photo next to their *L.104 Flugboot* (Floatplane) parked inside a hangar.

Flugboot (Floatplane) landing on the waters of the Adriatic.

This is a stunning photo of a Lohner "*Typ*/Type L" *L.38 Flugboot* (Floatplane) in flight over the *Flotte* (fleet) in the Adriatic.

A Lohner "*Typ*/Type L" *L.100 Flugboot* (Floatplane) in flight.

Naval aviators (*Seeflieger/piloten*) taking off from the waters of the Adriatic in their Lohner "*Typ*/Type L" L.50 *Flugboot* (Floatplane).

The *S.M.S. Lika* towing naval aviators (*Seeflieger/piloten*) in their Lohner "*Typ*/Type L" *Flugboot* (Floatplane).

"*Typ*/Type R" *R2 Flugboot* (Floatplane) parked on the waters of the Adriatic.

"*Typ*/Type G" *G2 Flugboot* (Floatplane) during take off.

A *Flugboot* (Floatplane) parked in the waters of the Adriatic.

Naval aviators (*Seeflieger/piloten*) in their "*Typ*/Type E" *E.21 Flugboot* (Floatplane) coming in for a landing.

Naval aviators (*Seeflieger/piloten*) in their "*Typ*/Type E" *E.37 Flugboot* (Floatplane) parked near the *S.M.S. Erzherzog Karl*.

Above: A *Flugboot* (Floatplane) coming in for a landing on the waters of the Adriatic. Below: With *Habsburgklasse Schacht Schiffe* (Habsburg Class Battleships) in the background, naval aviators (*Seeflieger/piloten*) sit in their "*Typ*/Type L" *L.70 Flugboot* (Floatplane) parked on the calm waters of the Adriatic.

Naval aviators (*Seeflieger/piloten*) parked in their *K.375 Flugboot* (Floatplane), Venice 1918.

K.375 Flugboot (Floatplane), Venice 1918.

K.195 Flugboot (Floatplane) on the Adriatic.

"*Typ*/Type E" *E.21 Flugboot* (Floatplane) coming in for a landing on the waters of the Adriatic.

Above: Naval aviator (*Seeflieger/pilot*) tending to the engine of his "*Typ*/Type *S*" *S4 Flugboot* (Floatplane) parked on the calm waters of the Adriatic. Below: Clad in their flight caps and jackets, two naval aviators (*Seeflieger/piloten*) and their crew pose for a photo with their "*Typ*/Type *E* " *E.18 Flugboot* (Floatplane) parked on the quiet waters of the Adriatic.

Above: Two naval aviators (*Seeflieger/piloten*) wearing flight caps with *Brille* (goggles) pose for a photo in the cockpit of their "*Typ*/Type *L*" *L.87 Flugboot* (Floatplane) parked on the Adriatic. Below: Two naval aviators (*Seeflieger/piloten*) seated in the cockpit of their "*Typ*/Type L" *L.105 Flugboot* (Floatplane).

Naval aviators (*Seeflieger/piloten*) seated in the cockpit of their *K.315 Flugboot* (Floatplane).

The wreckage of a Lohner "*Typ*/Type L" *L.56 Flugboot* (Floatplane).

A *K.199 Flugboot* (Floatplane) parked outside of a hangar, Triest 1916.

Naval aviators (*Seeflieger/piloten*) and crewmen pose for a photo with their *K.392 Flugboot* (Floatplane) parked outside of a hangar, Triest 1916.

A *Flugboot* (Floatplane) under construction.

A *K.392 Flugboot* (Floatplane) parked on a field near an aerodrome.

L.121 "Banfield" Flugboot (Floatplane) parked outside of a hangar.

Naval aviators (*Seeflieger/piloten*) pose for a photo with their "*Typ/Type*" *L.65 Flugboot* (Floatplane).

A "*Typ*/Type" *L.101 Flugboot* (Floatplane) parked on the calm waters of the Adriatic.

A "*Typ*/Type" *L.157 Flugboot* (Floatplane) parked inside a hangar at Pola.

Removing a *K.434 Flugboot* (Floatplane) from a hangar.

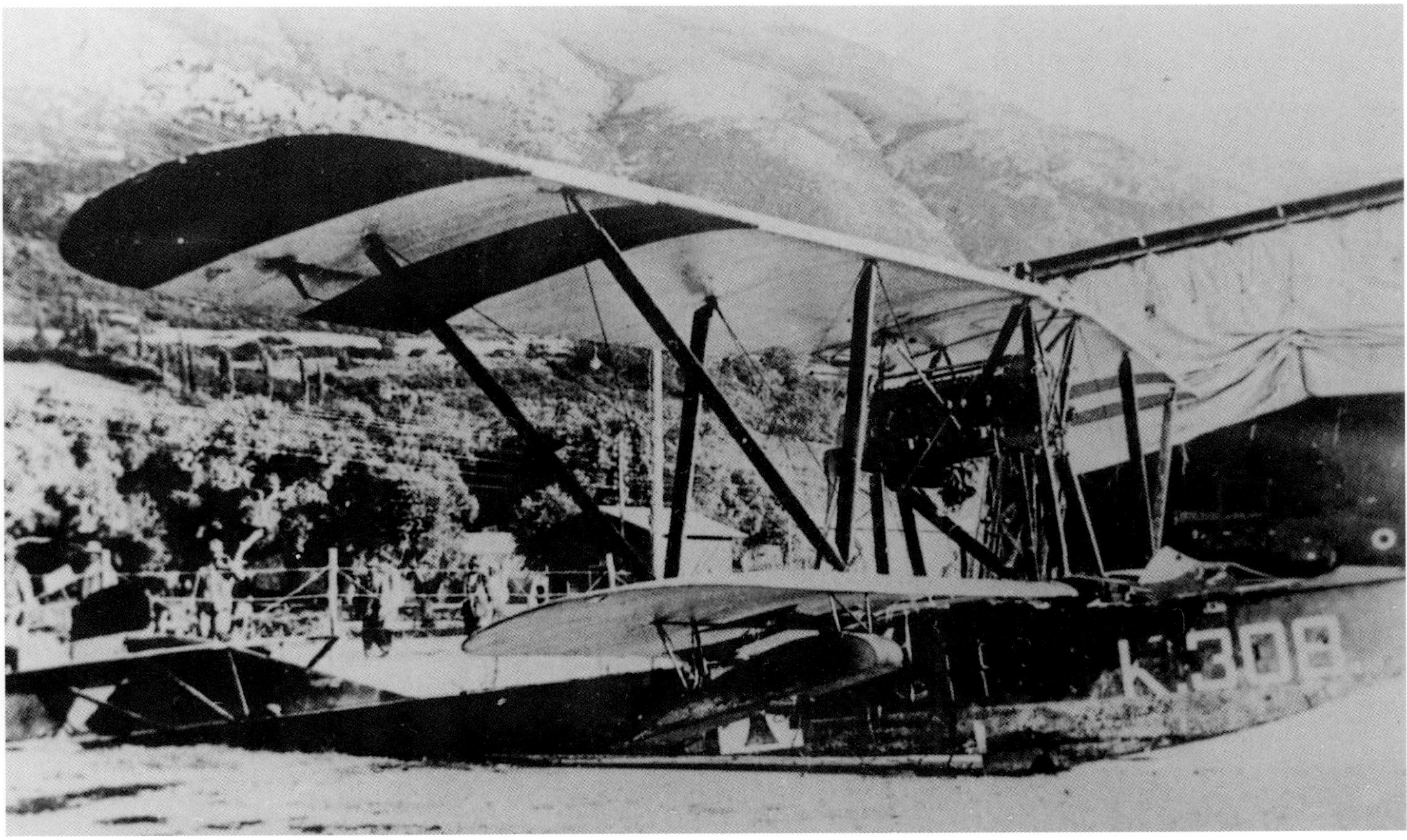

A *K.308 Flugboot* (Floatplane) after a rough landing, 1918.

Naval aviators (*Seeflieger/piloten*) leaving the cockpit of their Lohner "*Typ*/Type L" *L.88 Flugboot* (Floatplane).

Italian soldiers examining the wreckage of a "*Typ*/Type L" *L.138 Flugboot* (Floatplane).

G2 Flugboot (Floatplane) on the Adriatic.

Above: A naval aviator (*Seeflieger/pilot*) wearing a flight cap with *Brille* (goggles) poses for a photo with his "*Typ*/Type L" *L.138 Flugboot* (Floatplane). Below: A Lohner "*Typ*/Type L" *L.87 Flugbcot* (Floatplane).

A Lohner "*Typ*/Type L" *L.133 Flugboot* (Floatplane).

A "*Typ*/Type R" *R.301 Flugboot* (Floatplane) parked outside a hangar.

Two naval aviators (*Seeflieger/piloten*) pose for a photo with their canine companion inside a hangar next to their Lohner "*Typ*/Type L" *L.56 Flugboot* (Floatplane).

The wreckage of a *K.312 Flugboot* (Floatplane).

Above: Naval aviators (*Seeflieger/piloten*) and crewmen pose for a photo with their *G9 Flugboot* (Floatplane) parked outside a hangar. Below: *R.301 Flugboot* (Floatplane) under construction inside a hangar.

Two naval aviators (*Seeflieger/piloten*) wearing flight caps with *Brille* (goggles) pose for a photo seated in the cockpit of their "*Typ*/Type L" *L.96 Flugboot* (Floatplane).

Seated in the cockpit of their "*Typ*/Type L" *L.96 Flugboot* (Floatplane), two naval aviators (*Seeflieger/piloten*) wearing flight caps with *Brille* (flight goggles) pose proudly for a photo.

Above: A "*Typ*/Type L" *L.115 Flugboot* (Floatplane) on the waters of the Adriatic. Below: Three naval aviators (*Seeflieger/piloten*) pose proudly for a photo with their "*Typ*/Type L" *L.65 Flugboot* (Floatplane) parked on the beach.

Naval aviators (*Seeflieger/piloten*) pose proudly for a photo with their "*Typ*/Type E" *E.19* & *E.20* floatplanes parked inside a spacious hangar.

Servicing the engine of a "*Typ*/Type E" *E.21* parked inside a hangar.

This naval aviator (*Seeflieger/pilot*) poses proudly for a photo with his "*Typ*/Type L" *L.59 Flugboot* (Floatplane) parked on the beach.

Drachenballon (observation balloon), Pola.

A *S.26* in flight over the Adriatic with an *Erherzogklasse Schlacht Schiffe* (Erherzog Class Battleship) in the background.

Chapter Eight

Beamten
Civil Servants

Leaning on his saber, this mustached *Gendarme* poses proudly for a photo in a double breasted dark wool tunic and leather helmet with metal fittings. He has an intricately crafted "FJI" fastened to his helmet, and he has been decorated with *die Jubiläums Kreuze 1908* (The 1908 Jubilee Cross).

Five bearded and mustached *Beamten* (civil servants) wearing plumed headdress and double breasted dark wool uniforms pose for a pre- to early war vintage photo with their children.

The bearded *Beamte* (civil servant) in this cabinet portrait has a gilded and enameled badge (see Color Gallery) fastened above his right breast pocket. The badge is inscribed *K.K. Militär V. ReichsbundMit Gott für Kaiser u. Vaterland*. Detailed views of this genuine badge are in the Color Gallery.

This mustached *Beamte* (civil servant) poses proudly for a pre- to early war vintage cabinet portrait dressed in a privately tailored double breasted dark wool tunic with three decorations fastened to his chest. He has placed his headdress on an intricately carved table to his right. His collar insignia were referred to as *Semmel Stern. Semmel* is Southern German for *Brotchen* (roll/biscuit), and *Stern* is German for star.

The mustached *Beamte* (civil servant) in this studio photo wears a privately tailored double breasted wool tunic with decorations stitched to his chest. One of his decorations is *die Ehrenzeichen für Verdienste um das Rote Kreuz* (The Red Cross Award for Honorary Service).

The mustached *Beamte* (civil servant) in this cabinet portrait wears a privately tailored double breasted dark colored wool tunic with four medals fastened to his chest. He has *Semmel Stern* and gold-stitched winged wheel insignia stitched to his collar, indicating he is with the railroad (*Eisenbahn*).

Chapter Nine

Pre- to Early War

Twenty-two bearded and mustached *k.u.k Soldaten* (imperial and royal soldiers) pose for a pre- to early war vintage group photo outside of their barracks. Many have on the *Honvéd*/Hungarian style trousers referred to as *Magyarnadrág*.

Four *k.u.k. Soldaten* clad in pre- to early war period uniforms pose for a photo armed with their 8mm caliber bolt action *Steyr Mannlicher* rifles. All four are equipped with Model 1888 leather ammunition pouches.

This *k.u.k Soldat* poses proudly for a pre- to early war vintage photo holding his shako in his left hand.

Thirty-nine *k.u.k Soldaten* pose for a pre- to early war vintage photo dressed in a variety of headdresses and tunics. The soldier second in from the left in the second row wears a madder red wool fez, and in the same row (fifth in) is a soldier wearing a *Kommode Shako*.

Armed with 8mm caliber bolt-action *Steyr Mannlicher* rifles, this group of *k.u.k. Soldaten* from the *K.K. L.I.R. Nr 9, 13 Komp.* pose for a photo outside of a *Monturdepot* in *Wien* (Vienna).

K.u.k Soldaten wearing a variety of uniforms pose for a photo outside their barracks. Each is armed with an 8mm caliber bolt action *Steyr Mannlicher Gewehr.* The reverse side of this photo postcard is stamped *Mähr.Ostrau Moravska Ostrava.*

Twenty-five *k.u.k Soldaten* dressed in dark wool uniforms, and armed with 8mm caliber bolt action *Steyr Mannlicher* rifles, pose for a pre- to early war vintage photo in a field.

A group of twenty-one *k.u.k Soldaten* pause for a photo to commemorate their time in service. Many of these *Soldaten* have been awarded proficiency badges for artillerists.

Forty-one *k.u.k. Soldaten* wearing field caps and shakos pose for a photo to commemorate their time as recruits.

Above: In this pre- to early war vintage photo postcard, twenty-five *k.u.k Soldaten* from a mounted artillery unit pose proudly dressed in dark wool uniforms. Below: Eight *k.u.k Soldaten* appear ready for action with their 8mm caliber bolt action *Steyr Mannlicher* rifles. Six of these *Soldaten* wear depot issued field caps, and the other two wear caps that were privately purchased.

A group of *k.u.k Soldaten* pause for a pre- to early period photo dressed in various models of uniforms, and armed with 8mm caliber bolt-action *Steyr Mannlicher* rifles.

A group of *k.u.k Soldaten* pose for a photo wearing a variety of uniforms. Many wear summer weight white cotton pants, which were usually worn around the barracks or during training. Seated front and center are two mustached *Bosniaken* (Bosnians) wearing madder red wool fezzes.

Above: *K.u.k Soldaten* from a mounted unit pose for a photo with their canine friend while enjoying a drink and music. Below: With their *Zugführer* seated near the center, this group of *k.u.k Soldaten* pose for a pre- to early war vintage photo dressed in dark wool uniforms, and equipped with glass canteens encased in metal covers.

Above: Twenty-four *k.u.k Soldaten* from the *k.u.k Pionier Bataillon Nr.15 2.Komp.* pose for a studio photo. Many in this photo have been awarded proficiency badges for pioneers. Below: Two *k.u.k Soldaten* clad in depot issued wool field caps and overcoats pose for a photo in the hallway of their barracks with two of their *Kameraden* (Comrades) wearing shakos, and armed with 8mm caliber bolt-action *Steyr Mannlicher* rifles.

K.u.k. Soldaten wearing shakos with *hechtgrau* (pike gray) wool uniforms pose for a pre- to early war vintage photo armed with 8mm caliber bolt-action *Steyr Mannlicher* rifles, and equipped with Model 1888 leather ammunition pouches.

A group of *k.u.k. Soldaten* wearing shakos pose proudly for a photo with their regimental banner.

Above: The members of the *Wiener* (Viennese) *Hoch und Deutschmeister Kapelle* (Band) wearing shakos pose proudly for a photo with their instruments. Below: This group of *k.u.k Soldaten* pose proudly for a pre- to early war vintage photo wearing various styles of headdresses.

This mustached *k.u.k Soldat* poses proudly for a pre- to early war vintage studio photo with his shako resting on the table to his left.

Chapter Ten

Artillery

Two *k.u.k Soldaten* carefully aim an Ehrhardt System 8cm caliber Flak (*Flugabwehrkanone*). Flak cannons such as this one seen here were often mounted on truck beds.

A *k.u.k. Soldat* wearing a *Schiffchen* (forage cap) stares down the rifled barrel of his artillery piece.

Artillerists clad in feldgrau (field gray) uniforms preparing to fire their M.11 30.5cm Mörser (Mortar).

M.16 30.5cm Mörser (Mortar).

K.u.k. Soldaten clad in various models of uniforms pose proudly for a photo with their M.16 30.5cm Mörser (Mortar).

Loading a M.11 30.5cm *Mörser* (Mortar).

Two *k.u.k Soldaten* dressed in feldgrau (field gray) uniforms pose for a photo with a dummy artillery piece used for training, as well as to fool enemy forces.

A pre- to early war cabinet portrait of an artillerist wearing a dark brown wool tunic with proficiency badge. He has placed his *Kanonier* shako on the table to his right.

Chapter Eleven

Communication Units

Austro-Hungarian and German *Soldaten* (soldiers/troopers) in a *Brieftauben* (carrier pigeon) unit.

Above: Two telephone operators dressed in *feldgrau* (field gray) uniforms record and send messages using their Model 1907 field telephone. Below: A mustached telephone operator dressed in *feldgrau* (field gray) inside his bunker on the frontlines.

Above: Two *k.u.k. Soldaten* dressed in *feldgrau* (field gray) uniforms pose for a photo inside their barracks. The *Soldat* on the left holds the receiver to a Model 1907 field telephone. Below: A group of *k.u.k Soldaten* from a communications unit pose for a photo with some of their equipment.

Two telephone operators dressed in *feldgrau* (field gray) uniforms using their Model 1907 field telephone.

K.u.k. Soldaten dressed in *feldgrau* (field gray) uniforms erecting a telephone pole near the frontlines.

Chapter Twelve

The Kaisers and the Generals

Erzherzog (Archduke) Franz Ferdinand with his wife Sophie Chotek *Fürstin von Hohenberg* (Princess of Hohenberg), and their children Princess Sophie von Hohenberg, Maximilian, Duke of Hohenberg, and Prince Ernst von Hohenberg.

Kaiser Franz Josef I dressed as a *Honvéd*/Hungarian Hussar.

This photo postcard featuring Franz Joseph I wearing all of his medals and decorations was produced by the *Rotes Kreuz* (Red Cross) to support the war effort, 1916.

This is a photo postcard issued by the *Rotes Kreuz* (Red Cross) depicting His Majesty Kaiser Franz Josef with Archduke Franz Josef Otto, son of the Archduke Heir to the Throne.

Kaiserliche Königliche Österreiches Post/ Imperial and Royal Austrian Postal Service.

Above: Kaiser Franz Josef I and his entourage. Below: Kaiser Franz Josef I visiting with public dignitaries.

Kaiser Franz Joseph I and his mounted entourage.

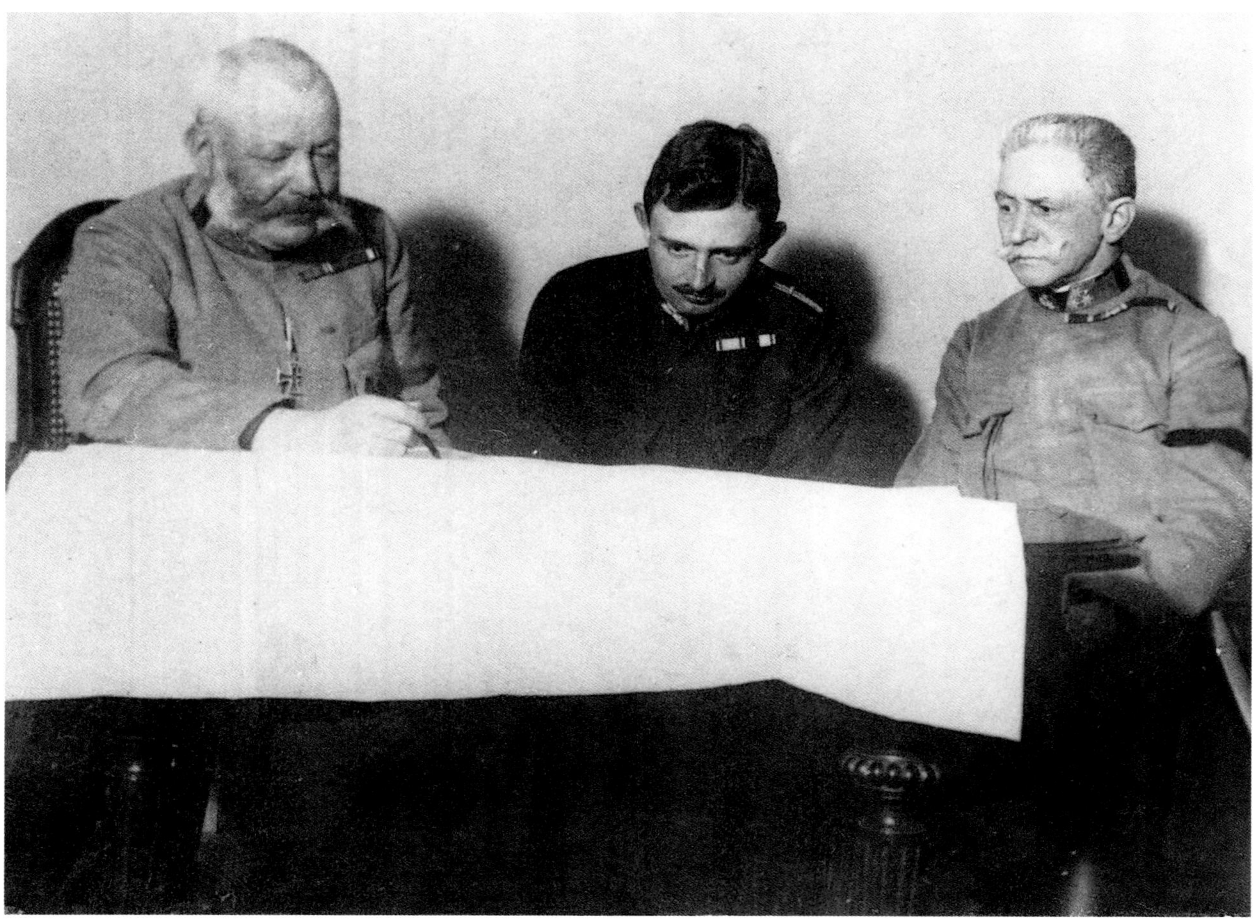

A candid photo of Erzherzog (Archduke) Friederich (left), Kaiser Karl (center), and Conrad von Hötzendorf (right).

Kaiser Karl with his entourage visiting the troops.

Standing on snow covered ground, Kaiser Karl, dressed in his Hussar uniform, poses for a photo with his entourage.

Above: Kaiser Karl visiting with a group of *Flieger* (aviators/pilots). Below: This aviator demonstrates for Kaiser Karl how a piece of equipment functions.

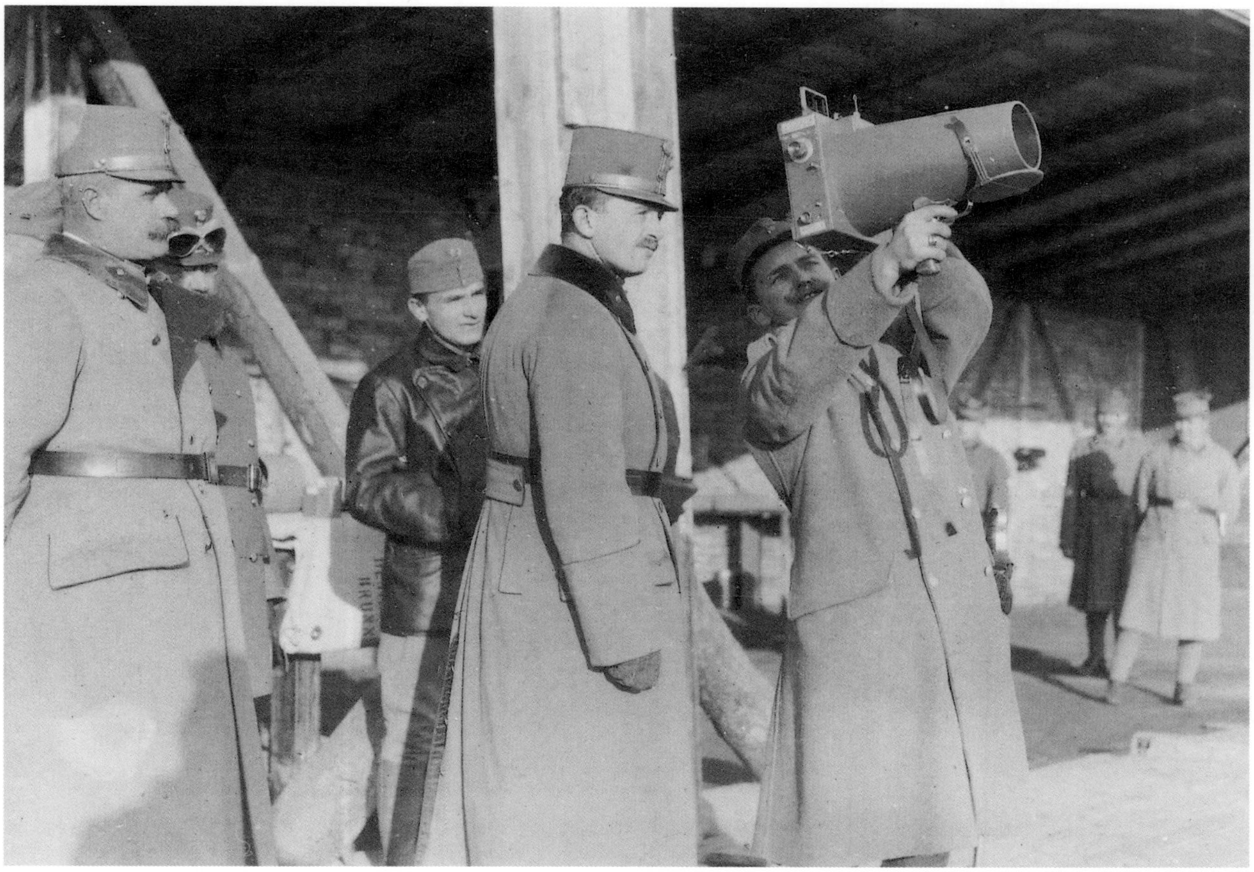

Kaiser Karl receives a demonstration of an aerial observation camera.

Visiting and greeting decorated *Tiroler Standschützen*.

Above: Prince Leopold von Bayern saluting members of the Austro-Hungarian *Generalstab* (General Staff). Prince Leopold was a veteran of the Austro-Prussian (1866) as well as the Franco-Prussian War. He was awarded the Order of Max-Joseph in addition to the *Eisernes Kreuz* (Iron Cross) first and second class. After having retired in 1913, he was recalled to duty in April 1915 and given command of the 9th Army. Below: *Generalstab* (General Staff) *am Bahnhof* (at the Train Station).

Generalstab (General Staff).

Austro-Hungarian and German *Generalstab* (General Staff).

August 1916.

Feldmarschall Eduard Freiherr von Böhm-Ermolli was an Italian born Austrian who was in command of the 2nd Army on the Eastern front.

Bulgaria

Chapter Thirteen

Machineguns

Three Bulgarian soldiers (*voinitzi*) pose for a photo with their belt fed machinegun (*kartechnitza*). Each wears a steel helmet (*kaska*) fashioned after Imperial German manufactured models.

Armed with either a rifle (*pushka*) or a Maxim machinegun (*kartechnitza*), this group of Bulgarian *voinitzi* (soldiers) poses for a photo wearing visor caps (*keppeta*) with cockades bearing the national colors of Bulgaria, which are white, green, and red.

This group of *voinitzi* (soldiers) poses proudly for a photo with their machinegun (*kartechnitza*). Each *voinik* (soldier) wears an overcoat (*Palto/Shinel*) and ammunition pouches (*patrondash*).

Each *moriak* (sailor) in this photo poses proudly wearing a *bushlat* (P-coat) and a cap with tally. They are armed with bolt-action rifles and a belt fed Austro-Hungarian manufactured *Schwarzlose*.

Nine *voinitzi* (soldiers) pose proudly for a photo with their belt fed Austro-Hungarian manufactured *Schwarzlose*. Each wears either a wool *Palto/Shinel* (overcoat) or *skala* (tunic).

Thirteen *voinitzi* (soldiers) stare into the sky looking for enemy aircraft. Their belt-fed *kartechnitza* (machinegun) is mounted for anti-aircraft use.

Seven *voinitzi* (soldiers) pose for a photo in a trench (*okop*) with their belt fed Maxim mounted on a tripod. Each wears a steel helmet (*kaska*) fashioned after Imperial German manufactured models.

Two mustached *voinitzi* (soldiers) pose for a photo with their belt fed Austro-Hungarian manufactured *Schwarzlose* mounted on a tripod. Each wears a *kaska* (steel helmet) and a dark colored wool *skala* (tunic).

Chapter Fourteen

Medical

A bearded *Sveshtennick* (regimental priest), *voinitzi* (soldiers), and *sestri* (nurses) from the *Cherven Krust* (Red Cross) pause for a photo in the field. The reverse side of this photo postcard is dated *15/VIII 1917*.

Above: *Sestri* (nurses) from the *Cherven Krust* (Red Cross) pose for a photo with their patients on and around the steps of a hospital. Below: Standing next to a pile of logs, and holding his walking cane in his right hand, this *voinik* (soldier) wearing a wool *skala* (tunic) poses for a photo near a *Cherven Krust* (Red Cross) medical station.

A group of medics (*sanitaren*) and wounded (*ranen*) pose for a photo near a church.

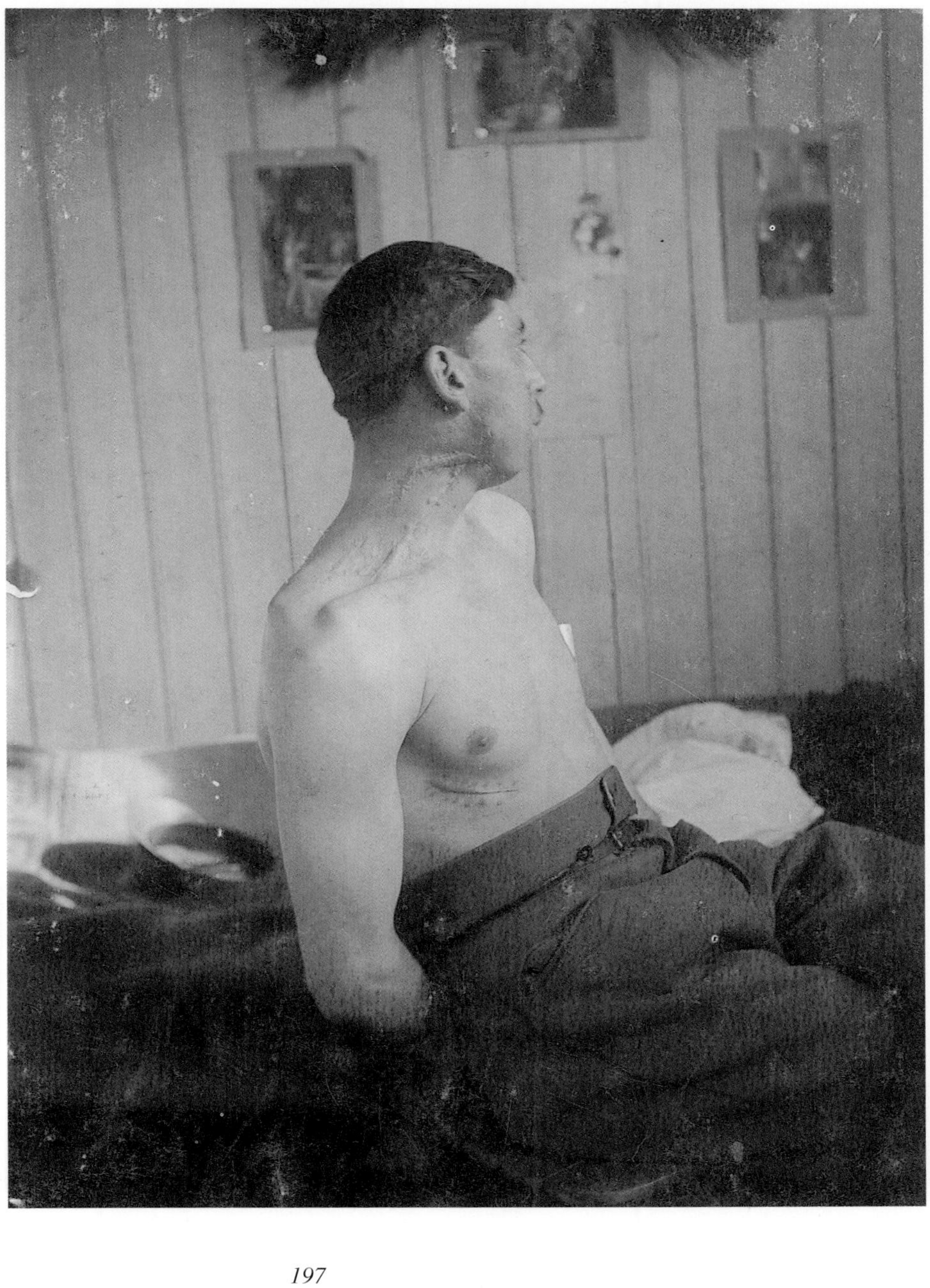

Seated on a cot inside his barracks, this brave *voinik* (soldier) displays his wounds. The reverse side of this photo postcard is stamped *15. X. 1917*.

Doctors, surgeons, and patients pose for a group photo outside of their hospital tent.

Eight mustached *voinitzi* (soldiers) pose for a late war vintage photo. The *voinik* (soldier) seated second on the left wears a *Cherven Krust* (Red Cross) brassard.

Above: A group of medics and wounded (*ranen*) camped in a village near the front. Below: Seventeen medics pose for a photo on the side of a hill before returning to the frontlines.

Above: A bearded *Sveshtennick* (regimental priest) with a Red Cross stitched on his left sleeve poses for a photo with two mustached officers outside of their quarters. Below: This *sestra* (nurse) dressed in white poses for a photo with her patients. The reverse side of this photo postcard is dated *27/IV 1917*.

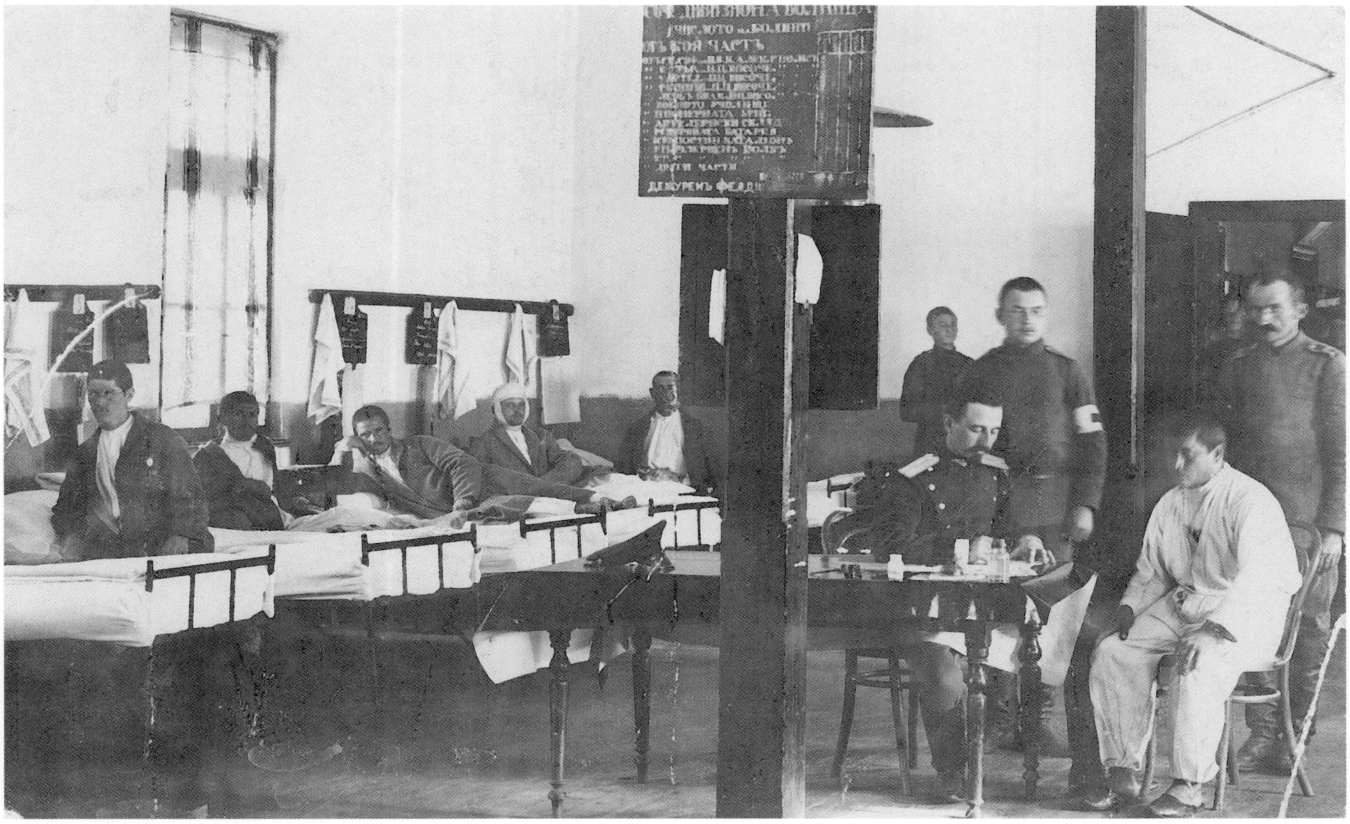

Patients and medics pose for a photo inside a hospital near the front lines.

A medical station set up in a wooded area near the frontlines.

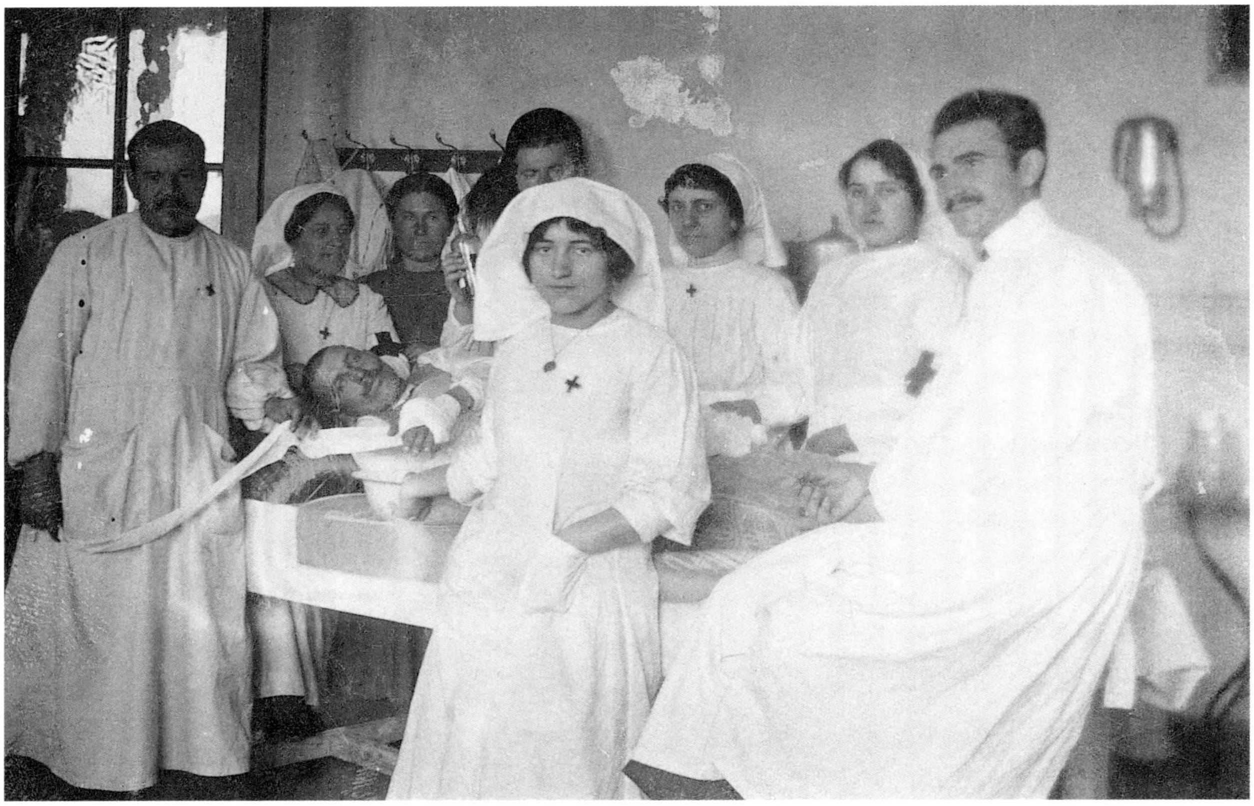

Above: *Sestri* (nurses) and *doctori* (doctors) from the *Cherven Krust* (Red Cross) pose for a photo with their patient inside an operating room. Below: In this oval shaped photo, five *voinitzi* (soldiers) pose wearing various models of tunics. Three of these *voinitzi* have a *Cherven Krust* (Red Cross) brassard on their left sleeves.

Chapter Fifteen

General Infantry

A bearded orthodox priest poses with four *voinitzi* (soldiers) outside a church decorated with religious icons. Each of these *voinitzi* wears a wool *skala* (tunic) based on the Models 1905 and 1909.

In this cabinet portrait, a bearded priest holding the hand of a civilian poses with a mustached officer wearing a pre- to early war style double breasted wool overcoat.

This unique photo features a young graduate (left), and a fully equipped *voinik* (soldier) armed with a bolt-action rifle and bayonet (right).

In this 1918 vintage photo postcard, four *voinitzi* (soldiers) pose for a photo on their way to a monastery in Ohrid, Macedonia.

In this cabinet portrait, a mustached *voinik* (soldier) who appears to have the rank of *poruchik* (lieutenant) poses proudly with his bride. In addition, he wears a white double breasted *skala* (tunic), and is armed with a Model 1889 saber (*sabja*).

Seven *voinitzi* (soldiers) clad in wool and linen tunics pause from eating their freshly carved watermelon for a photo. Two of the *voinitzi* have *Cherven Krust* (Red Cross) brassards on their left sleeves.

Two *voinitzi* (soldiers) pose proudly in this late war vintage studio photo armed with Model 1889 sabers. The *voinik* (soldier) on the left wears a Model 1908 tunic, and the *voinik* on the right wears a single breasted wool overcoat (*palto/shinel*). Each has a lanyard attached to their holstered side-arm.

This mustached *voinik* (soldier) poses proudly for a photo armed with a Model 1889 saber (*sabja*).

A group of *voinitzi* (soldiers) pose for a photo wearing *keppeta* (visor hats) with cockades and various models of tunics. The reverse side of this photo postcard is dated *20/III 1918*.

With his right hand in his pocket, this *voinik* (soldier) poses proudly for a photo wearing a *keppe* (visor cap) and a high-collared wool *skala* (tunic) with concealed buttons.

This *Sveshtennick* (regimental orthodox priest) poses for a photo with a group of *voinitzi* (soldiers) and *k.u.k. Soldaten* (imperial and royal soldiers).

Above: Twelve *voinitzi* (soldiers) dressed in either a cotton or wool *skala* (tunic) pause from their washing for a photo. Below: In this pre- to early war vintage photo a group of *voinitzi* (soldiers) wearing white *keppeta* (visor caps) and armed with bolt-action rifles watch a demonstration on how to fire a rifle from a tripod.

Three *voinitzi* (soldiers) wearing summer weight tunics and visor caps with cockades bearing the Bulgarian national colors (white-green-red) pose for a photo while relaxing on a hillside.

With small fish caught in nets, a group of *voinitzi* (soldiers) pause for a photo while floating in their canoes. The reverse side of this photo postcard is dated 1918.

A group of *voinitzi* (soldiers) clad in summer weight uniforms pose for a photo outside of their building.

In this pre- to early war vintage cabinet portrait, a mustached civil servant dressed in a dark colored wool *keppe* (visor cap) and overcoat (*palto/shinel*) poses with his female companion.

This photo postcard displays both summer weight (left) and all weather weight (right) uniforms available for *voinitzi* (soldiers).

This *voinik* (soldier) picking a flower for his sweetheart wears a Model 1908 *skala* (tunic) with *remak* (shoulder boards) and a decoration ribbon.

The dark haired *voinik* (soldier) in this 1918 vintage studio photo wears a *skala* (tunic) with a high collar and pleated breast pockets.

Three mustached *voinitzi* (soldiers) wearing Model 1905/1909 tunics with *remak* (shoulder boards) bearing rank distinctions pose for a photo while relaxing high up in the rocks. Each has a *kokarda* (cockade) bearing the national colors of Bulgaria (white-green-red) fastened to his visor cap.

Above: *Voinitzi* (soldiers) wearing wool Model 1905/1909 tunics pose for a photo with civilians outside of a dwelling. Below: A group of battle weary *voinitzi* (soldiers) clad in well worn tunics and overcoats pose for a photo alongside a stone wall.

In this late war vintage photo postcard, a group of *voinitzi* (soldiers) pose wearing various models of tunics and overcoats.

Three rugged looking *voinitzi* (soldiers) pose in a rustic setting with their canine companion. The *voinik* (soldier) on the right, who appears to have suffered a head wound, wears *tzarvuli* (traditional/national garb style footwear made of leather and cloth). This photo postcard displays the eclectic looks of the Bulgarian soldiers during the First World War.

Above: Twenty-one *voinitzi* (soldiers) clad in summer weight cotton and wool uniforms fashioned after the Models 1905/1909 pose proudly for a group photo. Five of the officers are armed with Model 1889 sabers. Sabers used by the Bulgarian armed forces were often manufactured abroad in such places as the Austro-Hungarian Empire or Imperial Germany. Below: Thirty-four *voinitzi* (soldiers) pose for a group photo outside of their building. Each *voinik* (soldier) wears a wool overcoat (*palto/shinel*) and belt (*kolan*). Two of the officers carry Model 1889 sabers.

Above: Cadets and civilians pose for a photo in a gated garden. Below: In this photo postcard, dated on the reverse side *8/III 1916*, eighteen *voinitzi* (soldiers) pose proudly in a studio. Each wears an overcoat (*palto/shinel*), and many are armed with Model 1889 sabers. The *voinik* (soldier) in the front row on the far left has a lanyard around his neck attaching to his holstered sidearm, and the *voinik* on the far right in the second row wears a *Cherven Krust* (Red Cross) brassard on his left sleeve.

Eight *voinitzi* (soldiers) wearing various styles of heavy winter wool overcoats pose proudly for a late war vintage studio photo. Flowers were usually given to new recruits or *voinitzi* furlough. Note the piping on the shoulder straps of the two *voinitzi* in the back row.

In this 1917 vintage cabinet portrait, two mustached *voinitzi* (soldiers) pose confidently. Goggles, such as the pair on the visor cap of the *voinik* (soldier) seated on the right, were preferred by aviators and motorists. Note the influence of Czarist Russian (*gymnastiorki, furashki*) and Imperial German models of uniforms on the uniforms these two *voinitzi* are wearing.

Three *voinitzi* (soldiers) wearing various models of uniforms made from different materials pose confidently for a photo by a stone wall. Walking sticks were a fashionable accessory during the First World War.

Three bearded *voinitzi* (soldiers) pose proudly for a studio photo wearing single breasted wool tunics and *keppeta* (visor caps). Ankle shoes with socks, such as the *voinik* (soldier) on the left is wearing, were sometimes worn instead of *botushi* (boots).

Two *voinitzi* (soldiers) wearing depot issued wool uniforms pose confidently for a late to post war vintage photo.

Clutching what appears to be a captured Czarist Russian saber, this mustached *voinik* (soldier) wearing an overcoat (*palto/shinel*) and visor cap (*keppe*) poses proudly for a late war vintage photo.

Wearing what appears to be a privately tailored uniform, this cloaked *voinik* (soldier) poses for a late war vintage studio photo holding his Model 1889 saber with his left hand. Piping often appeared on uniforms of *voinitzi* (soldiers) who were attached to special units.

Three *voinitzi* (soldiers) dressed in depot issued tunics with concealed buttons pose for a studio photo. The numbers on their *remak* (shoulder boards) indicate their unit.

Two *voinitzi* (soldiers) pose for a studio photo wearing cotton field blouses resembling a Czarist Russian *gymnastiorka*. Both have braided piping on their *remak* (shoulder boards), indicating they are most likely in either a guard, volunteer, or other special unit.

This mustached *voinik* (soldier) poses for a studio photo dressed in an overcoat (*palto/shinel*) made of a heavy grade of wool. The porcelain *kokarda* (cockade) on his *keppe* (visor cap) bears the national colors of Bulgaria, which are white, green, and red.

Three battle hardened *voinitzi* (soldiers) clad in various cuts and styles of tunics pose confidently for a late war vintage photo. The *voinik* (soldier) on the left wears a style of *skala* (tunic) that shows signs of Imperial German influence, and the *voinik* on the left wears an Imperial German belt buckle.

Three mustached *voinitzi* (soldiers) dressed in different styles of tunics and field caps pose for a photo in front of a stone and stucco structure. The reverse side of this photo postcard is dated *26/IV 1918*.

A mustached *voinik* (soldier) hard at work on his foot peddle lave.

This mustached *voinik* (soldier) clad in a well worn Model 1905/1909 *skala* (tunic) and *keppe* (visor cap) pauses for a photo before sounding an alarm bell.

Above: These two *voinitzi* (soldiers) relaxing and enjoying a drink use an ammunition crate as a table. Below: This mustached *voinik* (soldier) wearing a cotton *skala* (tunic) and wool *keppe* (field cap) is making cups and other objects with a hand operated lave.

Officers dressed in various styles of privately tailored uniforms pause for a photo before enjoying a meal inside their mess hall decorated with patriotic motifs.

A group of *voinitzi* (soldiers) pause for a photo while constructing a dwelling.

A mustached *voinik* (soldier) wearing a depot issued Model 1905/1909 *skala* (tunic) poses proudly in this photo postcard bearing Imperial German motifs, such as the eagle and Iron Cross. "*GOTT MIT UNS*" translates "GOD WITH US," and "*1914 WELTKRIEG 1916*" translates "World War 1914-1916."

This group of *voinitzi* (soldiers) pauses for a photo during a relaxing rowboat ride on a lake.

Above: Clad in various styles of uniforms, as well as civilian dress, a group of *voinitzi* (soldiers) pose for a photo in their rowboats on a placid lake. Below: This *voinik* (soldier) standing in a field in the countryside poses proudly for a photo with two of the local ladies. The reverse side of this photo postcard is dated *23-IX-17*.

A group of *voinitzi* (soldiers) and civilians standing on the side of the railroad tracks pose for a photo while awaiting the arrival of a locomotive.

Orthodox priests, *voinitzi* (soldiers), Imperial German *Soldaten* (soldiers), and other public dignitaries pose for a group photo outside of a building.

A group of *voinitzi* (soldiers) dressed in various models of uniforms and civilians pause for a photo in a town located near the frontlines.

This *voinik* (soldier), dressed in a privately tailored uniform, poses proudly in this late war vintage studio photo with his canine friend. He has unit insignia on his *remak* (shoulder boards), and spurs on his *bot-ushi* (boots).

Clutching his Model 1889 saber, this *voinik* (soldier) poses proudly for a cabinet portrait wearing a wool Model 1905/1909 *skala* (tunic) with *remak* (shoulder boards) bearing rank insignia.

The mustached *voinik* in this cabinet portrait wears a well worn depot issued wool *skala* (tunic) with *remak* (shoulder boards). The bars on his *remak* indicate his rank (*Starshi* = Sergeant).

This mustached *voinik* (soldier) holding his hand wears an overcoat (*palto/shinel*) made of a heavy grade of wool. He wears a lanyard around his neck attached to his holstered sidearm, and an adjustable leather strap most likely attached to a dispatch case. The porcelain cockade on his visor cap bears the national colors of Bulgaria (white-green-red).

Five *voinitzi* (soldiers) wearing *keppeta* (visor caps) with cockades smile for the camera while they amuse themselves with their mules.

Voinitzi (soldiers) clad in various styles of uniforms leading mules load down with supplies up a rugged mountain trail.

In this circular shaped photo, five *voinitzi* (soldiers) dressed in their barracks clothing strike relaxed and humorous poses.

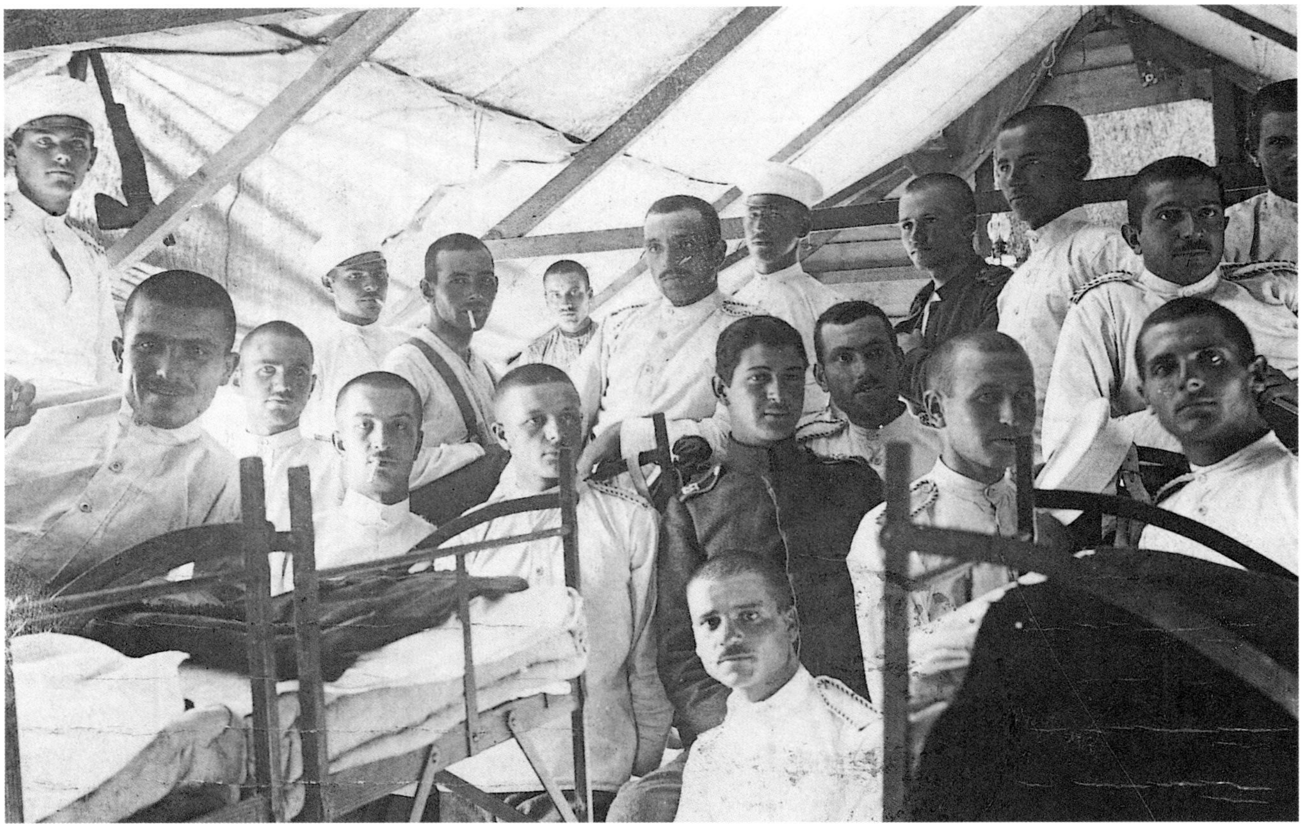

Above: A group of *voinitzi* (soldiers) dressed in wool and white summer weight uniforms pose for a photo on and around their bunks inside their tents. The reverse side of this photo postcard is stamped *28 VIII 1916*. Below: A group of *voinitzi* (soldiers) pose for a photo outside their tents. Each wears either a wool visor cap or a crushable white cotton cap. This photo offers a glimpse of what camp life was like for *voinitzi* during the First World War.

Three *voinitzi* (soldiers) pose confidently for a studio photo dressed in privately tailored tunics fashioned after the Models 1905 and 1909. The *voinik* (soldier) in the center has been decorated with a gilded and enameled military order for bravery.

In this studio photo pose two mustached enlisted rank *voinitzi* (soldiers) clad in late war period tunics and visor caps issued to them from a supply depot. The *voinik* (soldier) on the left is equipped with an Imperial German manufactured canteen with wool cover, and a dispatch pouch or binocular case with adjustable carrying strap.

The dark haired and mustached *ofitzer* (officer) in this souvenir cabinet portrait poses proudly with his bride. He is dressed in a double breasted white *skala* (tunic) with *remak* (shoulder boards), and armed with a Model 1889 *sabja* (saber).

Chapter Sixteen

Life on the Front and in the Trenches

Five *voinitzi* (soldiers) clad in wool uniforms pose for a photo outside of their *zemlyanka* (dugout/bunker), which they have given the name *Villa Anusha*, as the wooden sign hanging above the entrance indicates. The *voinik* (soldier) on the far left has been awarded the Iron Cross.

Seated outside of his tent dressed in a wool Model 1905/1909 *skala* (tunic), this *voinik* (soldier) pauses from his reading for a photo. This photo offers a glimpse of what camp life was like for the Bulgarian soldier during the First World War. The reverse side of this photo postcard is dated *16.IV.1917*.

Five *voinitzi* (soldiers) wearing wool field caps and tunics pause from repairing wagon wheels for a photo.

Above: Ten *voinitzi* (soldiers) clad in different models of uniforms made from various materials pose for a late war vintage photo. Below: In the south of Bulgaria, six *voinitzi* (soldiers) wearing wool field caps and tunics weave reed bottle covers. Reed bottle covers helped to prevent breakage while on the march. The reverse side of this very interesting photo postcard is dated *13/VII 1917*.

Fifteen *voinitzi* (soldiers) clad in various models of uniforms pose for a photo before boarding a train headed to the frontlines. Many of these *voinitzi* have porcelain cockades bearing the national colors of Bulgaria (white-green-red) fastened to their *keppeta* (visor caps).

Twenty-one *voinitzi* (soldiers) dressed in various models of uniforms pause for a photo and to drink a toast.

Three *voinitzi* (soldiers) pose for a photo inside their dwelling. The reverse side of this photo postcard is dated *8.IX.1918.*

These four *voinitzi* (soldiers) pause from playing their music for photo. Each wears an issued wool Model 1905/1909 *skala* (tunic) with *remak* (shoulder boards). The reverse side of this photo postcard is dated *28.V. 1918.*

Above: Three *voinitzi* (soldiers) dressed in depot issued tunics pose for a photo seated inside their bunker. The *voinik* (soldier) on the left wears *ersatz Pickelhaube* (spike helmet) made of pressed felt with a metal Prussian eagle. On their shelf they have placed a gasmask canister with carrying strap, *Cherven Krust* (Red Cross) rations, and other personal items. The reverse side of this photo postcard is dated *25/IX 1917*. Below: This mustached *voinik* (soldier) poses for a photo while relaxing on his bed inside of a bunker. He wears a wool *skala* (tunic), leather *kolan* (belt), and *keppe* (visor cap) with porcelain cockades bearing the Bulgarian national colors, which are white, green, and red. Hanging from the wood plank walls of the bunker are overcoats and gasmask canisters with carrying straps.

These fully equipped *voinitzi* (soldiers) armed with bolt action rifles (*pushka*) and stick grenades (*granati*) pose for a photo on the side of a hill before heading to the frontlines.

Southern front, 1917.

These *voinitzi* (soldiers) pose for a group photo dressed in different models of uniforms made of various materials. Many are armed with either a bolt-action rifle (*pushka*), pistol (*pistolet*), revolver, or bayonet (*shtik*). Several of these *voinitzi* have been decorated as well.

This group of *voinitzi* (soldiers) dressed in white *keppeta* (visor caps) and various model tunics poses for a photo.

Above: Two *voinitzi* (soldiers) wearing wool *keppeta* (visor caps) with porcelain cockades bearing the national colors of Bulgaria (white-green-red) examine their bodies. Below: A group of *voinitzi* (soldiers) enjoying a drink and relaxation at their hillside dwelling.

Three *voinitzi* (soldiers) dressed in various styles of uniforms pose for a photo while relaxing on a mountain.

Nine battle hardened *voinitzi* (soldiers) clad in different models of uniforms made of various materials pose for a late war vintage studio photo. The reverse side of this photo postcard is dated 1918.

These *voinitzi* (soldiers) are preparing lambs at their camp site.

A group of *voinitzi* (soldiers) and civilians repairing wagon wheels at a village near the frontlines. The reverse side of this photo postcard is dated 1917/1918.

Seven *voinitzi* (soldiers) dressed in various models of tunics enjoy a meal outside of their log bunker nestled in a forest. The reverse side of this photo postcard is dated 1918.

In a town near the frontlines, a group of *voinitzi* (soldiers) from various branches of the Bulgarian armed forces pose for a photo with a pig. The reverse side of this photo postcard is dated *11/XII 1918*.

Eleven *voinitzi* (soldiers) dressed in various models of tunics pose for a photo with *hulmove* (hills) in the background. Many carry either a walking stick or Model 1889 saber. Leather coats, such as the one the *voinik* (soldier) third in from the left is wearing, were preferred by motorists and aviators because of their exposure to the elements.

Forward observers on the southern front in 1917. This *voinik* (soldier) using his observation piece has placed his sidearm inside his *kobur* (holster).

This *voinik* (soldier) staring through the lenses of his observation piece wears a wool *skala* (tunic) and stiffened *keppe* (visor cap) with porcelain *kokarda* (cockade). The reverse side of this photo postcard is dated 1917.

Four *voinitzi* (soldiers) armed with 8mm caliber Austro-Hungarian manufactured *Steyr Mannlicher* Model 1895 rifles pose for a photo in a lightly forested area.

Above: Four *voinitzi* (soldiers) clad in field caps and tunics pose for a photo with their two canine friends. The reverse side of this photo postcard is dated 1917. Below: Gathered around a folding table made of wood outside of their tent, five *voinitzi* (soldiers) pause for a photo while engaged in conversation. Each wears a wool *skala* (tunic) with *remak* (shoulder boards) with rank insignia and *keppe* (visor cap) with porcelain *kokarda* (cockade) bearing the Bulgarian national colors (white, green, and red). The *voinik* (soldier) seated on the right wearing a Model 1905 *skala* has been awarded a military *Orden* (order) for bravery. The reverse side of this photo postcard is dated *20 VII 1916*.

Above: This *Sveshtennick* (Orthodox regimental priest) and group of *voinitzi* (soldiers) pose proudly for a commemorative photo with a brave comrade. On the reverse side of this photo postcard is an inscription and the date 1916. Below: A group of *voinitzi* (soldiers) piled on a horse-drawn wagon headed to the frontlines.

Two *voinitzi* (soldiers) wearing wool tunics and *keppeta* (visor caps) pose proudly in front of a log dwelling in a forested area.

Six high ranked officers dressed in privately tailored uniforms pose for a candid photo outside of a house near the frontlines.

Two *voinitzi* (soldiers) clad in well worn tunics pose for a photo with their canine friend.

A group of *voinitzi* (soldiers) dressed in *keppeta* (field caps) and tunics pose for a photo while drinking a toast.

Above: Five armed *voinitzi* (soldiers) wearing white *keppeta* (visor hats) and field blouses resembling Czarist Russian *gymnastiorki* pose proudly for a photo in their encampment. Below: Three mustached *voinitzi* (soldiers) wearing various styles of tunics and *keppeta* (visor hats) in different colors pose confidently for a photo outside of their dwelling. The reverse side of this photo postcard is dated *10/V 1916*.

Two mustached *voinitzi* (soldiers) wearing *keppeta* (visor hats) with porcelain cockades bearing the national colors of Bulgaria pose confidently for a photo outside of their log-reinforced dwelling. The *voinik* (soldier) on the left has a lanyard around his neck, which attaches to his holstered sidearm. The front of this photo postcard is dated in the lower right hand corner 29-10-1917, and the reverse side is dated *31.X. 1917*.

This *Sveshtennick* (orthodox regimental priest) poses for a group photo with eighteen *voinitzi* (soldiers) of various rank. These *voinitzi* wear various styles of privately manufactured tunics and visor caps.

Voinitzi (soldiers) and *k.u.k. Soldaten* (imperial and royal Austro-Hungarian soldiers/troopers) crossing a pontoon bridge on the Danube.

Three mustached *voinitzi* (soldiers) holding riding crops pose proudly for a late war vintage photo dressed in field caps and tunics.

Three *voinitzi* (soldiers) clad in various models of tunics pose for a photo while relaxing inside their tents.

In this 1916 vintage photo postcard, an orthodox priest gives mass for a group of *voinitzi* (soldiers).

A group of *voinitzi* (soldiers) and their wagons gathered near dwellings at the foot of a barren hill.

Above: Nine *voinitzi* (soldiers) clad in privately tailored tunics, as well as civilian dress, pose for a photo while relaxing outside of their tents. Two of these *voinitzi* (soldiers) are holding walking sticks and have been awarded Iron Crosses. Below: These *voinitzi* (soldiers) pose for a group photo dressed in early war vintage uniforms.

This mustached *voinik* (soldier) wearing a visor cap and overcoat (*palto/shinel*) with raised collar poses for a photo in a muddy field.

Three *voinitzi* (soldiers) pose for a photo outside of their dugout before enjoying a hot drink. All three wear leather *botushi* (boots).

In this 1918 vintage photo, seven *voinitzi* (soldiers) wearing various models and styles of field tunics and caps pose for a photo in a lightly forested area.

In this photo postcard dated *26/IV 1918*, a *voinik* (soldier) poses proudly wearing a summer weight *keppe* (field cap), tunic, and *pantaloni* (trousers), which he has bloused over his puttees. He has his holstered side-arm secured to his leather *kolan* (belt), as well as to a lanyard around his neck. His *voenni obuvki* (laced ankle/field boots) appear to be depot issued.

Two *voinitzi* (soldiers) wearing visor caps, cotton field blouses, and leather *botushi* (boots) pose for a photo holding their signal equipment.

Above: In this 1917 vintage photo postcard, two *voinitzi* (soldiers) equipped with binoculars pose for a photo inside their bomb shelter. Below: Five *voinitzi* (soldiers) clad in various cuts and styles of uniforms pose for a photo outside of their log dwelling.

Two Bulgarian officers in a wire basket being cabled up a mountain to an Austro-Hungarian position on the Italian front.

A bearded Bulgarian officer wearing a *palto/shinel* (overcoat) converses with an Austro-Hungarian officer wearing a *Mantel* (overcoat).

Above: The advancing 3rd Bulgarian Army Division (*Divisiya*), Dobrudscha. Below: *Voinitzi* (soldiers) mingling with the locals. The *voinik* (soldier) on the left holding his rifle (*pushka*) wears a traditional style of footwear native to the Balkans known as *opanci*.

Members of the High Command inspecting troops, 1917.

Members of the High Command pause for a photo next to their vehicle on a dirt road enroute to the frontlines, 1917.

Six decorated members of the High Command dressed in privately tailored uniforms pose for a photo outside of a cottage, 1917.

In this 1916 vintage photo, five members of the Bulgarian High Command dressed in privately tailored uniforms and one Turkish observer analyze terrain from an elevated position.

Members of the High Command planting a garden, 1917.

Members of the High Command clad in privately tailored summer weight uniforms inspect troops about to be deployed to the frontlines, 1917.

Decorated *voinitzi* (soldiers) greeting members of the High Command, 1917.

Members of the High Command salute a group off *voinitzi* (soldiers) as they march by, 1917.

Decorated members of the Bulgarian and Imperial German High Command pose for a photo in front of a monument located in a small town.

A group of *voinitzi* (soldiers) from various branches of the armed forces enjoying a theatrical performance, 1916.

A member of the Imperial German High Command awarding decorations to Bulgarian and German soldiers.

A Bulgarian officer proposing a toast before enjoying a meal with his comrades.

Saluting members of the High Command, 1917.

Five *voinitzi* (soldiers) pause for a photo with their spoked wheel vehicle parked on a sun drenched dirt road running alongside barbed wire entanglements. Seated in the vehicle are two members of the High Command. Each member wears a summer weight *skala* (tunic) and *tropicheski shlem* (tropical/sun helmet).

Seven members from the High Command observing terrain from an elevated position. Each member wears either a *keppe* (visor hat) or *tropicheski shlem* (tropical/sun helmet) with a porcelain cockade bearing the Bulgarian national colors fastened to the front.

Members of the High Command wearing either a *keppe* (visor) hat or *tropicheski shlem* (tropical/sun helmet) with a porcelain cockade bearing the Bulgarian national colors fastened to the front pause for a photo while conducting an inspection, 1917.

Members of the Bulgarian and Imperial German High Command salute a group of marching *voinitzi* (soldiers). White belts were usually worn by guards, or by *voinitzi* assigned to other special units.

Military press photographer preparing to take a photo of General Todorov, 1917.

Above: Members of the High Command and *voinitzi* (soldiers) from other ranks of the armed forces pose for a photo dressed in various models of uniforms. Below: Members of the High Command pause for a photo before enjoying a meal, 1917.

Bulgarian and Imperial German soldiers pose for a photo while enjoying a drink. Some of these soldiers have been awarded the Iron Cross.

A mustached Imperial German *Soldat* (soldier) wearing a *Pickelhaube* (spike helmet) with *Stoff Überzug* (cloth cover) poses for a photo with a group of Bulgarian *voinitzi* (soldiers).

Above: Seven *voinitzi* (soldiers) seated at a folding table outside of their tent pose for a photo. All seven have porcelain cockades bearing the Bulgarian national colors (white-green-red) fastened to their visor caps. The reverse side of this photo postcard is dated 1916. Below: A group of *voinitzi* (soldiers) clad in various models of uniform standing at attention.

A group of fully equipped *voinitzi* (soldiers) clad in various models of uniform standing at attention in a forest awaiting orders.

Southern front, 1916.

Two *voinitzi* (soldiers) pose for a photo alongside barbed wire fortifications. The *voinik* (soldier) on the right wears a wool overcoat (*palto/shinel*), while the *voinik* on the left wears a cloak.

Voinitzi (soldiers) carrying buckets down a trench. One of these *voinitzi* wears a steel helmet (*kaska*).

Above: A group of decorated *Shturmovi Voyski* (assault/storm troops) pose proudly for a photo while standing on a dirt road. Each is armed with a bolt-action rifle (*pushka*) and wears a steel helmet (*kaska*). Note one trooper has chosen to wear *tzarvuli* (traditional style of footwear native to the Balkans), while his comrades wear leather *botushi* (marching boots). Below: Six fierce looking *Shturmovi Voyski* (assault/storm troops) pose proudly for a photo armed with stick grenades. Each wears an Imperial German manufactured steel helmet (*kaska*), and is equipped with a gas mask (*protivogas*). The reverse side of this photo postcard is dated 1918.

Above: A group of *Shturmovi Voyski* (assault/storm troops) dressed in various models of uniform pose for a photo before returning to the battlefield. Below: An outstanding photo postcard capturing daring *Shturmovi Voyski* (assault/storm troops) in combat action! The reverse side of this photo postcard is dated *27 VII 1917*.

Standing outside of his dwelling holding a walking stick, this assault trooper poses proudly for a photo wearing a steel helmet (*kaska*) and a dark colored wool *skala* (tunic) with concealed buttons. He is armed with stick grenades and equipped with a *protivogas* (gasmask). The reverse side of this photo postcard is dated *20 X 1917*.

Chapter Seventeen

Artillery

A group of artillerists dressed in various models of uniform pose proudly for a photo with their *orudie* (field cannon).

Above: Dressed in summer weight uniforms, this group of artillerists poses for a photo with their foreign manufactured field cannons. Below: Six *voinitzi* (soldiers) dressed in overcoats, tunics, and visor caps pose for a photo with their *orudie* (field cannon) in a concealed position.

Above: Ten artillerists pose for a photo with their 75mm caliber Schneider field cannon. Below: Three artillerists dressed in wool uniforms pose for a photo with their 75mm *orudie* (field cannon). The mustached artillerist on the right has received two decorations, and has a lanyard around his neck attached to his holstered sidearm. The reverse side of this photo postcard is dated *20 IV 1918*.

Twelve Bulgarian *voinitzi* (soldiers) and two Imperial German *Soldaten* (soldiers) pose for a photo with their anti-aircraft cannon. The reverse side of this photo postcard is dated *25 IV 1917*.

While anticipating an enemy advance, this group of *voinitzi* (soldiers) pauses for a photo with their *orudie* (field cannon).

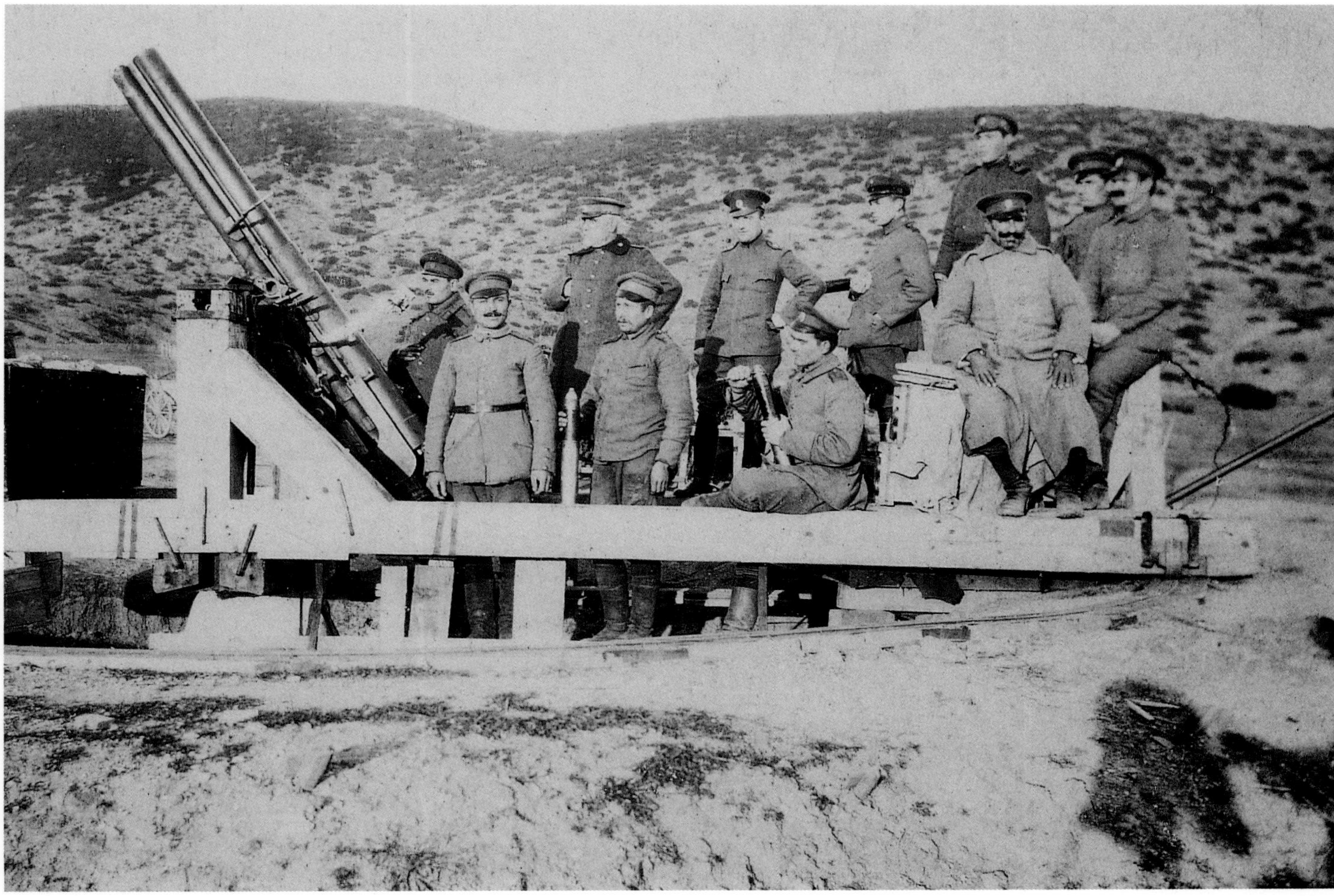

Eleven *voinitzi* (soldiers) dressed in various models of uniform pose for a photo with their anti-aircraft (*protivovazdushna*) cannon.

A group of artillerists pose for a photo with their *orudie* (field cannon). This photo postcard displays not only a breach view of the cannon, but also how projectiles were transported.

Six *voinitzi* (soldiers) pose proudly for a photo with their *orudie* (field cannon), which they have modified for use as an anti-craft (*protivovazdushna*) cannon.

Two artillerists pose for a photo with their *orudie* (field cannon), which they have mounted in a fortified position. This photo postcard is dated *25 VIII 1917*.

A group of artillerists clad in various models of uniform strenuously transporting their 75mm *orudie* (field cannon).

This group of artillerists pause for a photo while positioning their field cannons and caissons.

Artillerists preparing to fire, Southern front, 1917.

This group of artillerists pause for a photo after having fired their field cannon.

An outstanding photo of a cart/wagon used to transport winged/finned projectiles.

Nine *voinitzi* (soldiers) clad in various models of uniforms pose for a photo with winged/finned projectiles. The reverse side of this photo postcard is dated *21.III. 1918*.

Above: Eight *voinitzi* (soldiers) pose for a photo with various calibers of artillery projectiles. Projectiles were often transported in wicker casings, such as those featured here. Below: This *voinik* (soldier) wearing a stiffened visor cap stares at artillery projectiles while another *voinik* stands watch.

Seven *voinitzi* (soldiers) pose proudly for a photo with their *granatomet* (grenade launcher/*granatenwerfer*). Two of these *voinitzi* (soldiers) wear a steel helmet (*kaska*).

Chapter Eighteen

Unique and Unusual

Ten members of the territorial militia/frontier guard pose for a photo with their canine companions near a wooded area. Each wears *tzarvuli*, which is a style of footwear native to the Balkans. The reverse side of this photo postcard is dated *16.V. 1916*.

Three *voinitzi* (soldiers) pose for a photo while enjoying a drink from their wicker covered bottles. The *voinik* (soldier) armed with a double-barrel shotgun seated in the center wears a traditional Balkan style of footwear known as *tzarvuli*. The other two *voinitzi* wear issued leather *botushi* (marching boots).

This mustached *voinik* (soldier) relaxing on the ground wears a style of footwear fashioned after the national garb of the Balkans known as *tzarvuli*. He has belted his Model 1905/1908 wool tunic with an intricately stitched cloth *kolan* (belt). This style *kolan* was worn for gala dress, or when a *voinik* wanted to have a decadent appearance on the battlefield (a similar style belt and appearance can be seen in the bottom photo on page 154 of *Uniforms and Equipment of the Czarist Russian Armed Forces in World War I*). Tucked under his *remak* (shoulder boards) is a *bashlak* (hood/cowl) similar to the Czarist Russian *bashlik*. In addition, he is armed with a Model 1889 saber, and a sidearm with lanyard.

A team of fully equipped *voinitzi* (soldiers) crossing at a shallow point of water on spoke-wheel wagons. Note several of these *voinitzi* wear *tzarvuli*.

This group of *voinitzi* (soldiers) poses proudly on a wooden bridge spanning a calmly flowing river. These *voinitzi* wear either leather *botushi* (boots) or *tzarvuli*, which is a style of footwear native to the Balkans.

Two *voinitzi* (soldiers) wearing depot issued wool Model 1905/1909 tunics pose proudly for a photo postcard. The *voinik* (soldier) on the right wears cloth and leather *tzarvuli* (Traditional Balkan footwear), while his comrade on the left wears leather *botushi* (marching boots). Each has a porcelain cockade bearing the national colors of Bulgaria (white-green-red) fastened to his wool cap with leather visor.

This goateed *voinik* (soldier) wearing a *kalpak* (cylindrically shaped cap covered with fur/curly wool) bearing the Bulgarian coat of arms poses proudly for a pre- to early war vintage photo. Note the lion motif on the brass buttons of his single breasted *skala* (tunic), as well as the braiding bordering his *remak* (shoulder boards) with unit insignia.

Four *voinitzi* (soldiers) wearing wool tunics similar to the Model 1890 pose proudly for a pre- to early war cabinet portrait. Each wears a *kalpak* (cylindrically shaped cap covered with fur/curly wool) bearing the Bulgarian coat of arms, as well as leather *botushi* (boots).

A group of *voinitzi* (soldiers) wearing winter uniforms crossing through a snowy forest on horse-drawn wagons and sleighs.

A group of *voinitzi* (soldiers) from various branches of the Bulgarian armed forces pose proudly for a group photo dressed in different styles of uniform.

Nine young cadets pose for a pre- to early wartime photo with their canine friend.

Two *voinitzi* (soldiers) pose for a photo in a wooded area. Both of the *voinitzi* wear *tzarvuli* made of cloth and leather. The reverse side of this photo postcard is dated *I/VI 1918*.

Five *voinitzi* (soldiers) armed with M95 bayonets pose for a photo on a grassy clearing in a wooded area. The *voinik* (soldier) seated on the left brandishing the bright blade of his M95 *shtik* (bayonet) wears *tzarvuli* made of cloth and leather.

This mustached *voinik* (soldier) clad in an issued uniform and holding a bugle poses proudly for a cabinet portrait. He wears traditional *tzarvuli* made of cloth and leather. This cabinet portrait captures the rugged, yet elegant simplicity of a Bulgarian *voinik* during the First World War.

Chapter Nineteen

Medals, Decorations, and Orders

This goateed officer poses proudly wearing a privately made visor cap with metal and enamel cockade, as well as a double breasted overcoat (*palto/shinel*) with brass buttons bearing a lion motif. He has been awarded a white and red enameled Austro-Hungarian Military Service Cross (*k.u.k. Militärverdienstkreuz*), which he has fastened around his neck with a red and white silk ribbon concealed by the velvet collar of his overcoat. He has also earned the Imperial German Iron Cross, as is evidenced by the black silk ribbon with white stripes fastened to the button of his overcoat. He is armed with a Model 1889 saber and a holstered sidearm, which is fastened to a lanyard and unique style of belt.

Above: An orthodox priest poses for a photo with a group of *voinitzi* (soldiers) dressed in various styles of uniform at their encampment. Several of these *voinitzi* have been awarded military bravery medals, as well as Imperial German Iron Crosses. The reverse side of this photo postcard is dated 1917. Below: This goateed *voinik* (soldier) wears a privately tailored Model 1905/1908 *skala* (tunic) with *remak* (shoulder boards) bearing unit insignia. He has been awarded an enameled military bravery decoration and a Prince Ferdinand I Order of Merit 1887-1891.

This mustached *starshi* (sergeant) poses proudly for a studio photo with a military merit decoration fastened to his pre- to early war style single breasted *skala* (tunic).

This mustached *voinik* (soldier) wears a privately tailored *skala* (tunic) with concealed buttons and *remak* (shoulder boards). He has been awarded an enameled Royal Order of Alexander, as well as an Imperial German Iron Cross. In addition, he has a porcelain cockade bearing the national colors of Bulgaria (white-green-red) fastened to his visor cap.

Above: Five *voinitzi* (soldiers) pose for a photo dressed in various models and styles of wool tunics. Three of these *voinitzi* have been awarded military merit medals. The reverse side of this photo postcard is dated 1917. Below: Nine *voinitzi* (soldiers) pose proudly for a photo wearing different models of uniform as well as decorations, such as the Gallipoli Star (*Eiserner Halbmond* in German and *Harp Madalyasi* in Turkish), Iron Cross, and other military bravery and merit orders.

Three mustached *voinitzi* (soldiers) dressed in white double breasted tunics pose for a photo armed with Model 1889 sabers. Both *voinitzi* standing on the left and right have been awarded 1908 Bulgarian independence commemorative crosses (*1908 Vaspominatelen Krust*). The *voinik* (soldier) seated in the center, as well as the *voinik* standing on the left have been awarded enameled military orders for bravery.

These five *voinitzi* (soldiers) decorated with merit medals pose proudly for a photo wearing different model uniforms.

In this cabinet portrait, a mustached *voinik* (soldier) wearing a double breasted wool tunic with brass buttons bearing a lion motif poses proudly with his female companion. He has been awarded an enameled military bravery decoration, and a Prince Ferdinand I Order of Merit 1887-1891. In addition, he is armed with a Model 1889 saber. The reverse side of this cabinet portrait is dated *I/III/1918*.

This mustached *voinik* (soldier) poses proudly for a studio photo wearing a double breasted dark wool *skala* (tunic) with *remak* (shoulder boards). He has been awarded an enameled Military Bravery Medal with crossed swords.

In this remarkably detailed cabinet portrait, a mustached *voinik* (soldier) poses confidently before the camera while he clutches his visor cap and Model 1889 saber. He has an enameled Military Bravery Medal with crossed swords fastened to his privately tailored wool *skala* (tunic) with concealed buttons and double breast pockets.

In this superbly detailed cabinet portrait, a highly decorated *voinik* (soldier) poses confidently wearing a gala dress uniform.

A fabulously well focused and detailed photo of General Major Daniel Nikolaev wearing a gala dress uniform with his medals, orders, and decorations.

Chapter Twenty

Other Units

Eight *voinitzi* (soldiers) dressed in various styles of wool uniform pose for a photo with their field telephones and bicycles.

Above: Inside a station near the frontlines, five *voinitzi* (soldiers) pause for a photo while receiving orders on their field telephones. The reverse side of this photo postcard is dated *19 IX 1918*. Below: Clad in various models of tunics, these *voinitzi* (soldiers) pose for a photo while receiving and recording orders coming in on their *polevi telefon* (field telephone). The reverse side of this photo postcard bears an ink unit stamp, as well as the date *13 V 1917*.

Above: Six *Svarzochni voiski* (signal troops) pose for a photo displaying various types and models of equipment. The reverse side of this photo postcard is dated 1917-1918. Below: Seven *voinitzi* (soldiers) clad in various models of tunic pause for a photo while calling on their *polevi telefon* (field telephone).

Thirteen *voinitzi* (soldiers) on horseback pose proudly for a photo dressed in various models of uniform. This photo postcard is dated *19-I-1918*.

A group of *voinitzi* (soldiers) on horseback wearing winter uniforms pose for a photo while riding through snow covered terrain.

Infantry, cavalry, and mounted members of the High Command pose for a late war vintage photo postcard.

A group of *voinitzi* (soldiers) on horseback pause for a photo.

Nine *voinitzi* (soldiers) on horseback wearing privately tailored double breasted wool overcoats pose for a photo near a body of water.

Members of a military marching band pose for a photo. The reverse side of this photo postcard is dated *25/XII 1917*.

Voinitzi (soldiers) dressed in various styles of uniform pose for a photo near the wreckage of a British biplane.

A group of *voinitzi* (soldiers) pose proudly for a photo with their captured British pilot.

These *voinitzi* (soldiers) wearing different styles of tunic pose for a photo with their canine friend and searchlight mounted on rails. The reverse side of this photo postcard is dated 1917.

A group of *voinitzi* (soldiers) and canine companion pose for a photo with a searchlight and other equipment.

Above: Members of a military marching band pose proudly for a group photo holding their instruments. Below: An outstanding pre- to early war vintage photo of Bulgarian hussars/guardsmen and civilians.

In this remarkably detailed oval photo, a hussar/guardsman poses confidently with his white gloved hands resting on his Model 1889 saber.

Chapter Twenty-one

Czars and Generals

A profile shot of Czar Ferdinand in full gala dress.

The Crown Prince Kirill and Prince Boris pose for a photo by the Black Sea before visiting the troops and the front.

Members of the Austro-Hungarian, Bulgarian, Imperial German, and Ottoman Turkish Command pose for a photo during a parade. The reverse side of this photo postcard is dated 1918, and has an ink stamp from Bucharest.

Members of the Austro-Hungarian, Bulgarian, and Imperial German Command wearing gala dress uniforms, as well as various medals, orders, and decorations.

A fabulously detailed and focused photo of General Major Radko Dimitriev in full gala dress.

Color Gallery

Forward and reverse views of the four pocket Model 1916 summer weight tunic (Bulgarian: *Skala* German: *Rockl/Jacke*) made of a late war *ersatz* type material. This style of tunic was worn by *k.u.k Soldaten* (imperial and royal Austro-Hungarian soldiers) as well as *voinitzi* (Bulgarian soldiers).

Interior of the four pocket Model 1916 summer weight tunic with reinforced stitching. Note the detailed shots of the loops on this tunic. The loops on the pocket held a breast badge.

Forward, reverse, and interior views of a pre to early war vintage Austro-Hungarian manufactured dark blue wool tunic (*Rock*) with *Papageigrün* (parrot green) collar, cuffs and trim tailored for *Generalmajor*. This tunic has braided and stitched gold cording on the cuffs referred to as "bear paws". The decorations on the tunic include a military service cross II (*Militär Dienstabzeichen II*), enameled military service cross (*Militär Verdienstkreuz*) with swords, and jubilee commemorative medal (*Jubiläumserinnungsmedaille*). Note the revealing image of the sash with clamp belonging to this tunic.

Forward, reverse, and side views of an identified Austro-Hungarian sailor shirt (*Matrosenhemd*). This model of *Matrosenhemd* was for seamen (*Matrosen*) 2-4 Class (*2-4 Klasse*) and boiler men (*Heizer*). Note the location of the stamp near the adjustment strings. Many imperial and royal navy (*K.u.k. Kriegsmarine*) items were stamped *M.B.A* (*Marine Bekleidungs Amt*).

Dark blue wool cap (*Kappe*) with tally (*Band*) for seamen (*Matrosen*) in the imperial and royal Austro-Hungarian navy (*k.u.k Kriegsmarine*) and other period naval regalia. Soldiers in other branches of the Austro-Hungarian armed forces prized cap badges (*Kappeabzeichen*) with naval motifs as well. The seashell featured here is a souvenir from the 1913 Adriatic Exhibition in Vienna. The 1916 vintage notepad bears a gold *k.u.k Kriegsmarine* seal.

Hechtgrau Schiffchen (pike gray forage cap) made of a fine grade of wool with gold-stitched Franz Joseph I cockade. Note the interior as well as the unit number six.

Feldgrau Schiffchen (field gray forage cap) made of a fine grade of wool. Note the Kaiser Karl cockade.

Forward, reverse, side views of a flight cap made in Vienna (*Wien*). Note the detailed view of the label and interior lining. Motor corps troops also preferred this style of headdress.

Forward, reverse, side views of a lined leather cap worn by aviators and motor corps drivers. Caps such as this one were issued or purchased privately by soldiers.

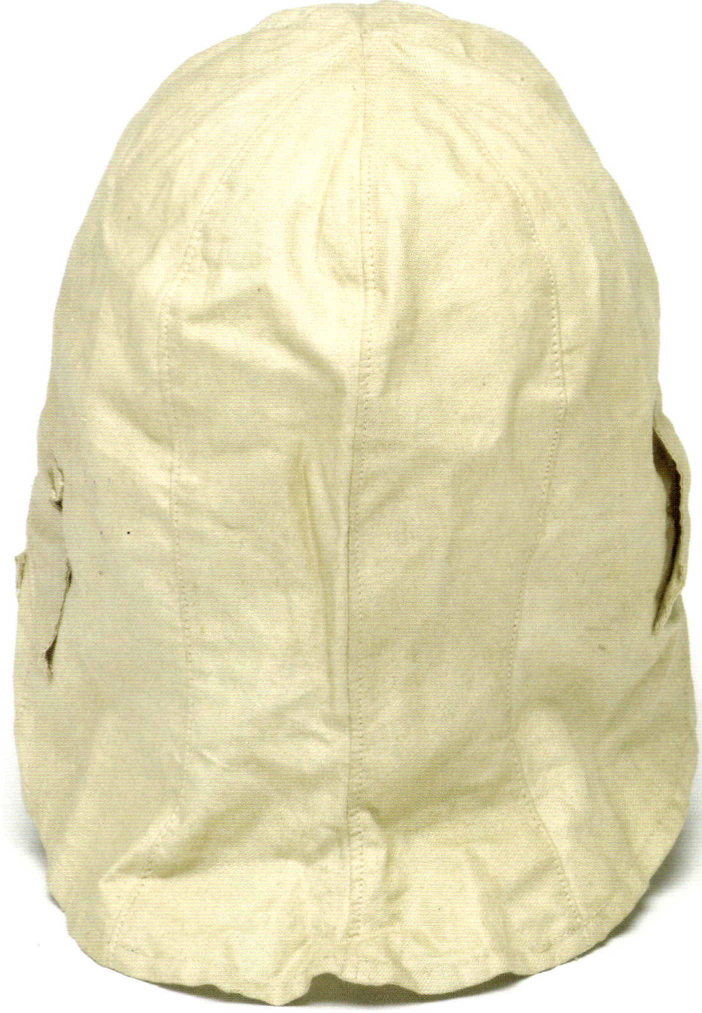

Light weight cloth cap with adjustable strap worn by aviators and motor corps drivers. The light color of this cap made it suitable for warm climates as well as for winter camouflage.

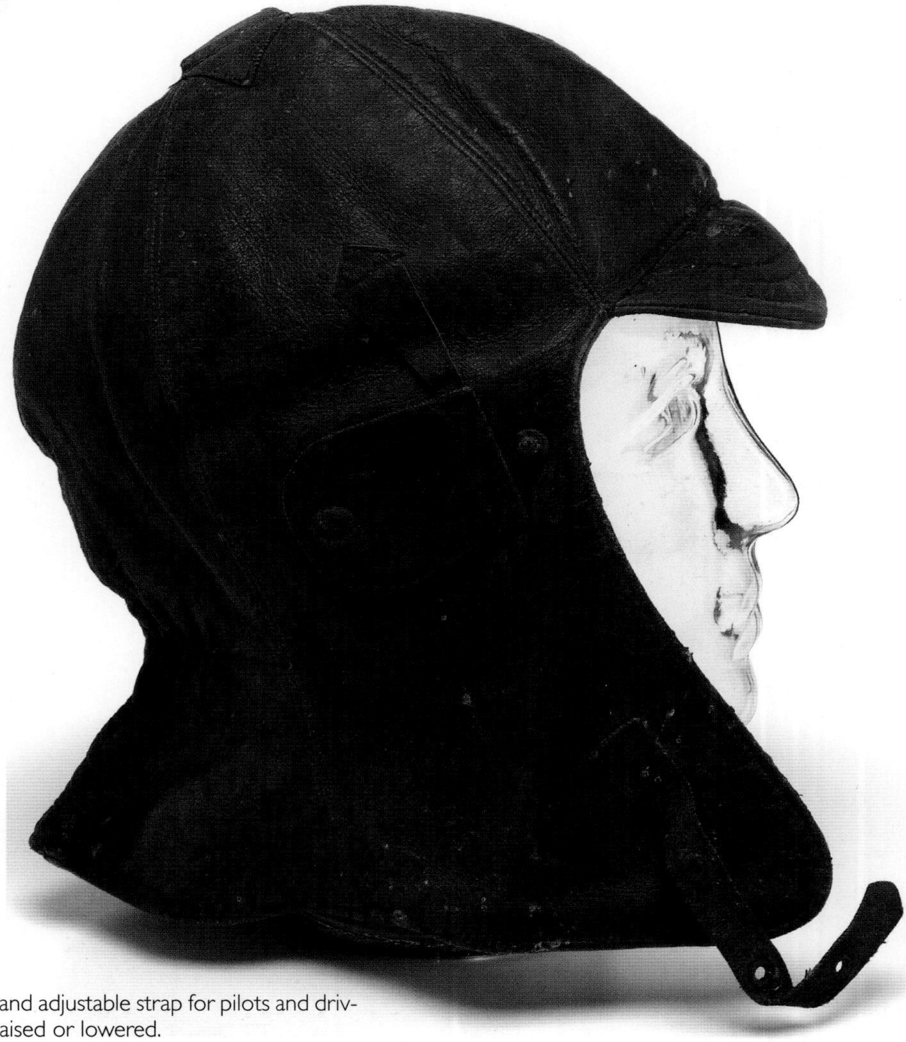

Lined leather cap with visor and adjustable strap for pilots and drivers. Note the visor can be raised or lowered.

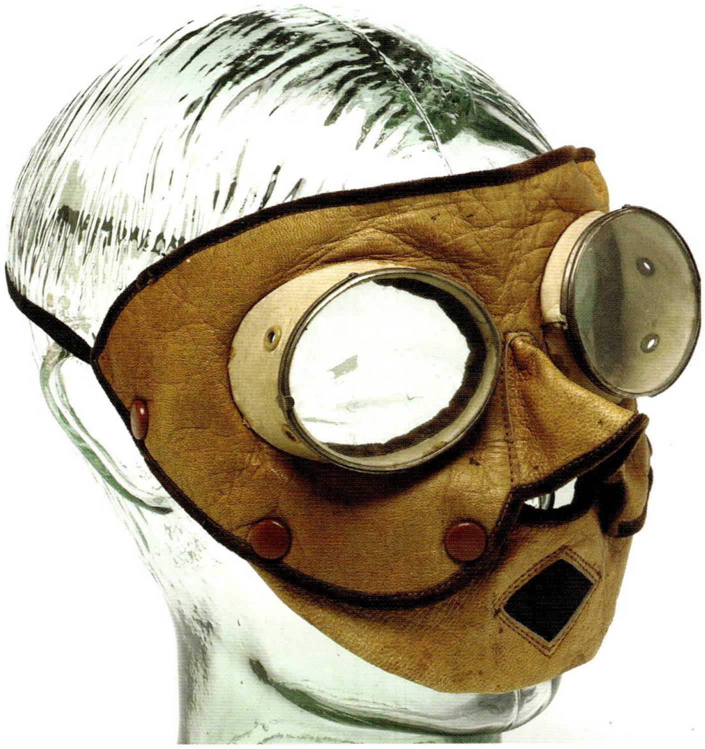

Three models of adjustable leather flight masks. Note the different shapes of lenses.

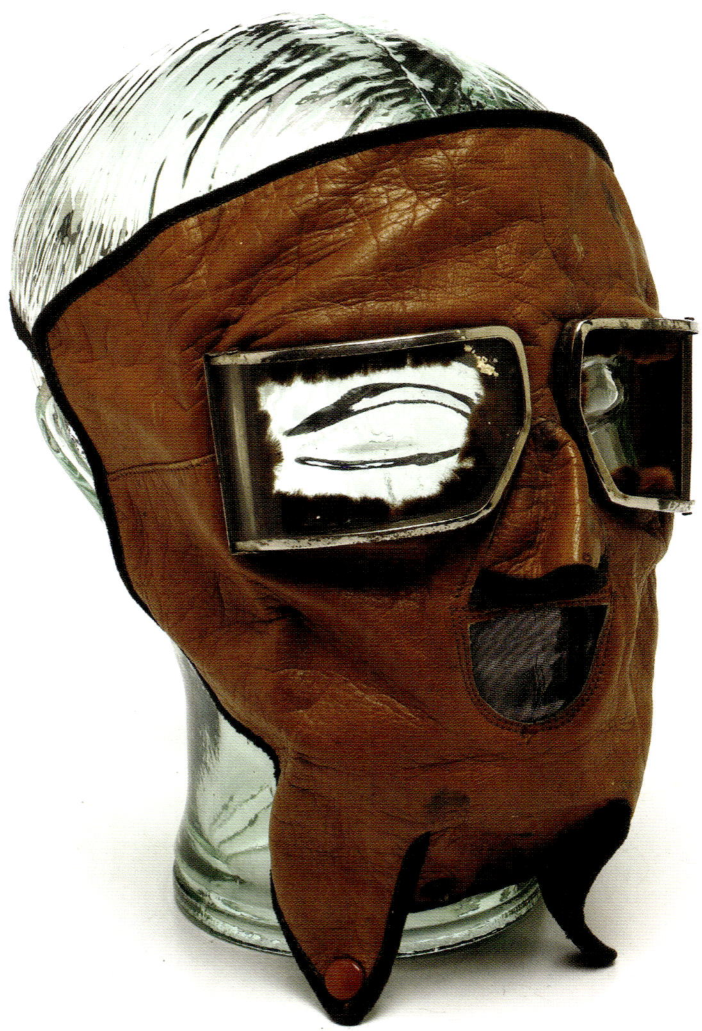

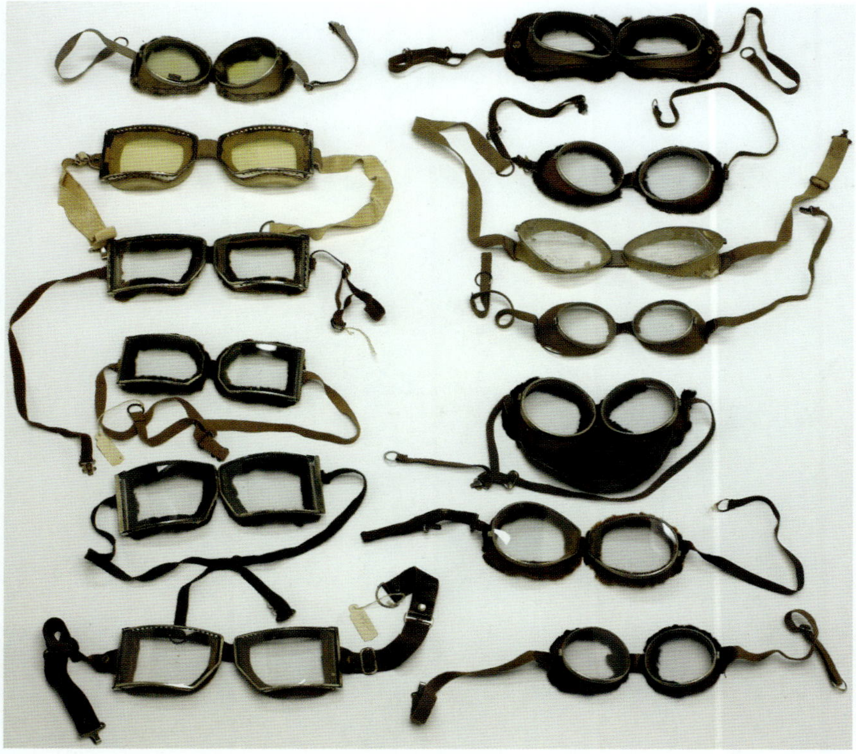

Left: Various models and styles of goggles worn by the armed forces.

Below: Row 1 - Field gray (*feldgrau*) wool collar (*Kragen*) with Austro-Hungarian *Generalmajor* insignia. After the war, many of the same tunics were used by national and paramilitary armed forces only with different collars and other slight modifications. Note how this *Kragen* is reinforced with burlap. Row 2 - Forward and reverse views of Austro-Hungarian *Feldwebel* collar patches with edelweiss insignia. Row 3 - Green felt collar patches with stitched edelweiss insignia. Collar patches without star insignia indicated enlisted rank Austro-Hungarian *Jäger* (hunter), Pioneer, *Trainsoldat* (e.g. soldier in a dog transport team), *Infanterist* (Infantry), *Kanonier*, or *Sanitätssoldat* (medic). Row 4 - From left to right forward and reverse views of sequined *Eisenbahn* (railroad), stitched edelweiss and stamped metal *Radfahrer* (bicyclist) collar insignia. Note this Eisenbahn insignia is an unused matching pair.

Above right: Various models of cloth Austro-Hungarian armbands/brassards (*Armbinden*). *Armbinden* were worn in the field as well as on maneuvers. Note the various fasteners and stitching. Above and Below: Two of many styles of period footwear worn by the armed forces. (Top) Laced leather boots with two buckle protective flap. This style of boot was preferred by aviators and motor corps troops. (Bottom) Laced leather ankle boots with field gray colored cloth lining. Note the wooden pegs in the soles.

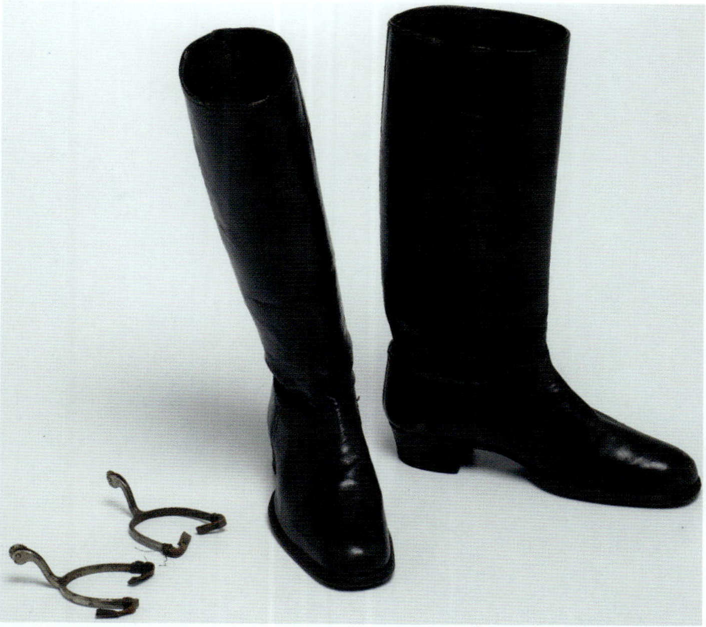

Above: Period black leather riding boots and spurs worn by the armed forces.

Below: Austro-Hungarian manufactured tin canister (*Dose*) for shoe polish (*Schuhcreme*) from the Black and Yellow Cross (*Schwarz-Gelbes Kreuz*). Black and Gold are the colors of the Habsburg monarchy. Right: Period advertisement for an imperial and royal court distributor. The ad reads *Only Schmoll Paste for Your Shoes!*

Forward, reverse, and interior views of two pre to early war models of depot issued haversacks. Note the stitching and metal fittings.

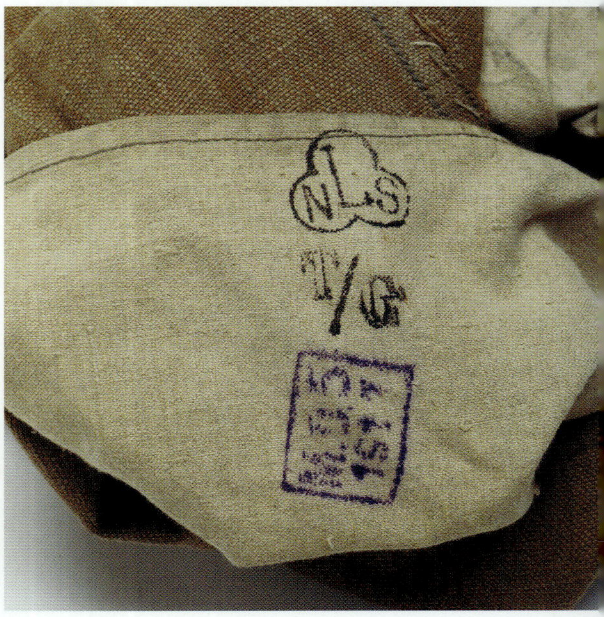

Forward, reverse, and interior views of two mid to late war models of depot issued haversacks. Note the close up view of the depot stamps on the haversack on the left.

Forward, reverse, and interior views of a pre to early war model lined calf-skin backpack with leather straps and metal fittings. Note the close up view and location of the depot stamps.

Forward, reverse, and interior views of modified backpacks.

Right: Leather belt and metal buckle with doubled headed eagle crest for enlisted rank troops. Below: Forward and reverse views of a belt buckle bearing an oak and laurel leaf motif as well as initials of Franz Joseph I (*FJI*). Upper ranks preferred this style of belt buckle.

Top: Metal and wood utensil set used by the armed forces. Note how each piece fits together. Middle: Foldable utensil set in leather carrying case. This type of utensil set was privately purchased by soldiers. Bottom: Fork (*Gabel*) and spoon (*Löffel*) from the imperial and royal military medical school (*k.u.k. Militärärztliche Schule*). Note the hallmarks.

Above: *Feldgrau Feldflaschen* (field gray canteens). Note the various enamel finishes as well as stamps and dates. This is the same model of canteen seen on the soldier who is featured on the cover (lower left image) and on page 57 in *Uniforms and Equipment of the Austro-Hungarian Army in World War One* from Schiffer Publishing. Below: Forward and reverse views of a Model 1909 aluminum canteen created into commemorative trench. This canteen was carried in various ways such as inside the haversack or in a leather harness. For period images displaying this model of canteen, see pages 56 (upper image), 66 and 122 (soldier on the far right, upper image) in *Uniforms and Equipment of the Austro-Hungarian Army in World War One* from Schiffer Publishing.

Stein made from an artillery round. Note the arsenal stamps on the bottom. Pitcher holder made from an artillery round and grenade parts. Note the intricate coat of arms on the front.

Drink ware with patriotic Kaiser motifs. The three metal cups referred to as *Kriegsbecher* (war tumbler/cup) were often engraved.

Three hand-painted regimental pipes bearing various motifs and expressions.

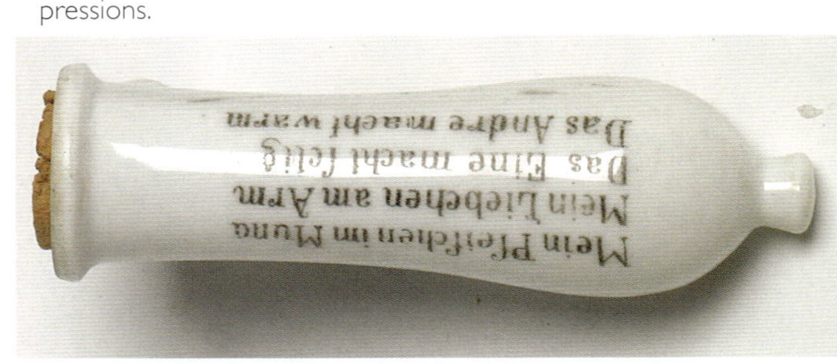

Theatre made general purpose storage tin with edelweiss motif.

Period (*left*) pocket watch in protective case with patriotic colored silk and metal fob, (*center*) leather wristwatch holder, and (*right*) wristwatch.

K.u.k Tobakdosen (imperial and royal tobacco tin containers) and *Zündholzschachtel* (matchbox).

Left: Gold embossed case for Austrian military veterans. Right: Period studio portrait of a mustached *k.u.k. Soldat* wearing featured badge.

Forward and reverse views of a gilded and enameled imperial and royal Austrian veterans badge with the inscription *MIT GOTT FÜR KAISER u. VATERLAND* (With God for emperor and fatherland) manufactured by Zimbler.

Pocket mirror bearing an image of *General Conrad von Hötzendorf*.

Forward and reverse side views of *General Conrad von Hötzendorf* commemorative disks (*Medaillen*).

Forward and reverse views of three variants of identification document containers for upper ranked *k.u.k Soldaten* and *Hónved* troops. These items were worn like dog tags and were referred to in German as *Legitimationsblattkapseln*.

Identification papers contained inside the featured *Legitimations-blattkapseln* and two enlisted (*Mannschaft*) troop variants.

Period personal items of a soldier.
1. Red colored leather bill holder with the gold seal of the imperially and royally privileged Austrian International Bank in Vienna, First District 3 Hohenstaufen Lane (*Kais. Kon. Privilegirte Österreichische Länderbank in Wien I Hohenstaufengasse 3*). 2. Czarist Russian and Italian currency in case of capture. 3. August 1914 dated twenty mark bills (*Zwanzig Markschein*), twenty crown (*Zwanzig Kronen*), two (*Zwei*) and one (*Eine*) crown (*Kronen*) bills all stamped *DEUTSCHÖSTERREICH*. Pebbled leather wallet with alpaca monogram. 4. Period spectacles with gold embossed leather carrying case made by an imperially and royally appointed court optician. 5. Twenty and ten cent Austrian coins (*Münzen*) with war year dates. 6. 1916 Calendar from the Red Cross. 7. Fine toothed comb made of bone. 8. Field post (*Feldpost*) box (*Schachtel*). Folded field post letter containing edelweiss flowers from the battleground. 9. Period playing cards. 10. Period bottle opener. 11. Foldable map of Southern Tyrol (*Südtirol*) marked *K.u.k. Theres. Militär-Akademie* in the upper corner. 12. Gold embossed leather covered document for wife and children. Patriotic glass bead work with war year dates displaying the Hungarian coat of arms and crown of St. Stephen (*Szent István*). 13. Service manual on *Sturmanriff* (assault attack)

Manuals and booklets foldout charts on the Czarist Russian and Italian armed forces. Such manuals were critical to the survival of Central Powers because of the detailed information provided. 1. *Die Russische Armee* (The Russian Army) this is a fascinating manual dated 1913 containing 173 pages with foldout maps and color plates detailing uniforms and regimental banners. 2. *Kurze Zusammenstellung über das russische Heer Dezember 1916* (Short Synopsis over the Russian Army December 1917). This manual shows signs of use by the soldier. It contains 253 pages many of which contain notes from the soldier who also wrote his name in the manual. There are color plates included as well. 3. *Kurze Zusammenstellung über die Russische Armee in Europa (ohne Kaukasus)* (Brief Conspectus over the Russian Army in Europe (excluding the Caucasus)) This manual is dated 1913 and includes 45 pages of text with colored plates. 4. *Die Russische Armee* (The Russian Army). This manual is dated 1913 and includes text with colored plates. 5. *Die Russische Armee Anfang 1917. Nur für den Dienstgebrauch.* (The Russian Army beginning 1917. Only for service use. This fascinating manual is dated 1917 and contains 286 pages of text, charts and color plates. 6. *Handkarte des gesamten Russischen Kriegsschauplatz 1915.* (Map of the entire Russian theater of War 1915). Highly detailed full color map of the Russian front in 1915. 7. *Gesänge russischer Kriegsgefangener im August und September 1916.* (Songs of Russian Prisoners of War in August and September of 1916. This is a fascinating 62 page study examining the songs and music of the multi-ethnic Czarist Russian armed forces. Such studies offered an insight on the morale of soldiers. 8. *Die Italiensche Armee* (The Italian Army). This is a manual documenting the Italian armed forces in 1913. 9. *Die Italiensche Armee* (The Italian Army). A wartime field manual issued to frontline troops.

Pre to war time service and instruction manuals with foldout charts. Manuals were as valuable to soldiers as their actual equipment. For military historians, such manuals are authentic primary resources. 1. *Instruction über die Einrichtung und Verwendung des Repetier Gewehres M. 95.* (Instruction on the Equipment and Usage of the M.95. Rifle). This manual is 88 pages long with foldout color charts. 2. *Vorschrift für die Verwaltung und Verrechnung der Armatur und Gewehrmunition.* (Regulations for the Administration and Clearing of Armature and Rifle Ammunition). This is a fascinating 174 page manual with detailed charts. Note the K.u.K. Munitions-Fabrik Wöllersdorf stamp. 3. *Instruction für die M. 12 B.u.St.mit 80cm Basis Distanzmesser (provisorisch).* (Instruction for the M. 12 B.u.St. with 80cm base distance measurer / range finder (provisional)). This is 51 page hand written instructional manual for a range finder. *Provisorisch* (provisional) indicates the instructional manual was temporary and subject to future modifications and additions. 4. *Anleitung für den Gebrauch des Handlüfters M.15* (Directions for the use of the Model 1915 hand operated ventilator). This manual is dated 1916 and contains instructions on how to use and maintain a Model 1915 hand operated ventilator. Ventilation of dugouts was very important for the survival soldiers during the First World War. Such ventilators came in useful when soldiers trapped inside of a dugout due to a cave in or bombardment needed air because it was easy to transport. 5. *Weisungen für die Verwendung von Santitätshunden, zugleich Tagebuch für Santitätshundeführer* (Instruction for the Use of Medical Canines/Dogs serving at the same time as a Journal for Medical Canine/Dog Guides). This is a *1916* dated 113 page journal and instruction manual for dogs use in medical units. This manual was heavily used by the owner and has multiple unit stamps throughout. 6. *Die Summerschalter* (The Buzzer Switch). This is 1917dated manual detailing the use of a buzzer switch for field telephones. 7. *Telegrapheninstruktion für die Armee im Felde* (Telegraph Instructions for the Army in the Field). An eighty page instruction manual. 8. *Scheinwerferunterricht* (Searchlight Instruction Course). This is a 1918 dated 226 page manual with foldout diagrams of equipment. 9. *Übersicht über die A.S. (Azetylen Sauerstoff) A Scheinwerfer, A Beleutungsmitel und A.S. und Signalgeräte.* (Outline over the A.S.(Acetylene Oxygen) and Acety-

Row 1 *Weihnachten im Felde 1916* (Christmas in the Field 1916) commemorative plaque made of *Erbeutetes Ital. Geschützmaterial* (plundered Italian artillery material) mounted on a piece of granite. Note the *11.Armee Tirol 1916 Abzeichen* (11th Army, Tyrol 1916 badge) as well as the signatures. Row 2 (*left*) Hand carved wood *Weihnachten 1915* (Christmas 1915) commemorative box bearing the profiles of both Kaisers. (*right*) Metal case with *Weihnachten im Felde 1916 Abzeichen* (Christmas in the Field 1916 badge). This motif also appeared on *Kappeabzeichen* (cap badges) as well. Row 3 (*left*) *Weihnachten im Felde 1916* (Christmas in the Field 1916) booklet with 1917 calendar and foldout maps. This particular booklet was used as a detailed journal. (*right*) Three *Kappeabzeichen* (cap badges) commemorating *Weihnachten im Felde* (Christmas in the Field) during the war years. Note the rare *Panzerzug* cap badge featured.

Row 1 Patriotic rings with war year dates. Row 2 Various styles of *Gold gab ich für Eisen 1914* rings (I gave gold for iron. 1914). These bands were given to soldiers and their wives if they surrendered their gold weddings rings for the war effort. Row 3 Patriotic ring bearing the profiles of both Kaisers. Row 4 The round cardboard boxes read *Struggle through to victory. A souvenir of the World War. 1914.* Each box houses one *Kriegsglück-Ring* (war luck ring/ lucky war ring) made from a horseshoe nail (*Hufnagel*). The paper that came with the ring explains what it signifies.

Following page: Row 1 (*left*) Forward and reverse views of a gilded and enameled cap badge for *Tiroler Landesschützen.* (*right*) Forward and reverse views of a silvered and enameled cap badge for *K.K. Landesschützenreg. No.III 1914-17.* Row 2 (*left*) Forward and reverse views of a metal cap badge for *Italienische Front Olasz-Front 1915-17* (*right*) Forward and reverse views of a metal cap badge for *Isonzo Armee.* Row 3 (*left*) Forward and reverse views of a metal cap badge with Papal motif and war year date. (*right*) Forward and reverse views of a metal cap badge for *ARZTL. (ärztlich) WAFFENBRL. (Waffenbrüderlichkeit) TAGUNG BADEN 11.13.X 1917* (Medical Brotherliness in Arms Conference in Baden 11.13.X 1917.) Row 4 (*left*) Forward and reverse views of a metal cap badge for Bulgarian *voinitzi* (soldiers) (*right*) Forward and reverse views of a metal cap badge for *XII. Korps Lemberg-Chyrow-Pilicia-Bug-Szczara-Jankow-Prusiecko-Iwangorod-Baranowiczy.* Row 5 (*left*) Forward and reverse views of gilded and enameled Austro-Hungarian rank insignia. (*right*) Forward and reverse views of metal edelweiss cap insignia. Note the enameled Slovakian coat of arms with argent patriarchal cross.

ITALIENISCHE FRONT
OLASZ-FRONT 1915-1917
ISONZO-ARMEE
1916
XII.KORPS
LEMBERG-CHYROW — PILICA-BUG-SZCZARA
JANKOW-PRUSIECKOJ WANGOROD BARANOWICZY

Forward and reverse views of a plaque made by *Kriegsgefangener* (Prisoners of War) in Siberia. The front of the plaque reads *Neither hope to win or to flee. Prisoner of War Camp Beresowka, Siberia.* The reverse side reads *In memory of captivity.*

Forward and reverse side views of a distance observer proficiency badge (*Distanzschätzauszeichung*).

Forward and reverse side views of a rare and detailed fob for *Honved Infanterieregiment 30*. Note the leather fastener.

Above: Forward, reverse and side views of an assault troop badge (*Sturmtruppabzeichen*). Note this badge fits the loops on the breast pocket of the Model 1916 tunic featured in this color gallery.. Below: Forward, reverse and side views of an assault troop badge (*Sturmtruppeabzeichen*) for *4J.D. Sturmtruppe*.

Two assault troop rings (*Sturmtruppringe*).

Forward and reverse views of a dagger/knife made from grenade parts with bone grip bearing assault troop motifs.

(Top left) Forward and reverse views of an aviator badge (*Fliegerabzeichen*) from *JASTA* 72-74 with *Adler* (eagle) and *Maschinengewehr* (machinegun) motif. Note *JASTA* stands for *Jagdstaffel*. (Bottom left) Forward and reverse views of a gilded and enameled *Fliegerabzeichen* (Pilot badge) lapel pin. (Top right and bottom right) Forward and reverse views of pin back eagle badges worn by aviators.

Two variants of darts/fleschettes used by aviators during the First World War. Pilots threw these from their cockpits while flying over targets. For a period image displaying fleschettes see Chapter Four page 70 in *Uniforms and Equipment of the Austro-Hungarian Army in World War One* from Schiffer Publishing.

Forward, reverse, and side views of a wind gauge/meter recovered from a plane.

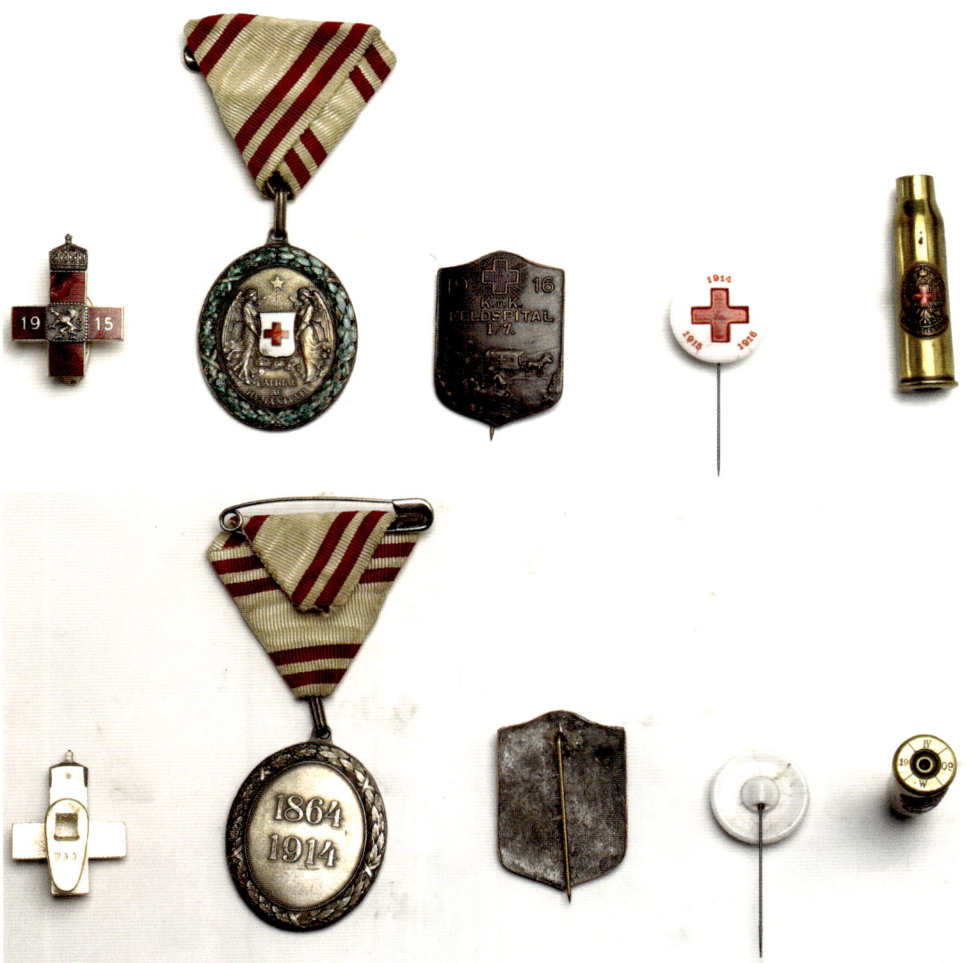

Row 1 Forward and reverse side views of an enameled Bulgarian *Cherven Krust* (Red Cross) badge. Row 2 Forward and reverse side views of an Austro-Hungarian 1864-1914 silvered and enameled *Roten Kreuze* (Red Cross) *m.d. K.D. mit Lorbeerkranz* (with laurel leaf wreath). Note the triangular white and red silk ribbon. Row 3 Forward and reverse side views of a metal cap badge for *1916 K.u.K Feldspital (Field hospital) 1/7.* Row 4 Forward and reverse side views of a ceramic Red Cross pin with war dates worn by Central Powers troops. Row 5 Forward and bottom views of a brass rifle shell casing with Austro-Hungarian Red Cross motif.

(left) Cardboard box from the Austro-Hungarian Red Cross (*Roten Kreuze*) which contained *Federhalter* (feather holders) costing *I Krone* (I Crown) a piece. Many an Austro-Hungarian soldier wore a feather (*Feder*) in his *Feldmütze* (field cap) especially if he was *Kaiserschützen.* A classic period image displaying this practice can be seen in *Chapter Seven* on page 121 of *Uniforms and Equipment of the Austro-Hungarian Army in World War One* from Schiffer Publishing. The field cap this soldier wears appears to be issued from a depot like the cap featured on page 329 in the Color Gallery of that volume and therefore he does not need a feather holder because the are two loops on the side. Note this period image appears on the back of the cover as well. (right) Wound tag. Medics tagged wounded soldiers and gave instructions for treatment and transport.

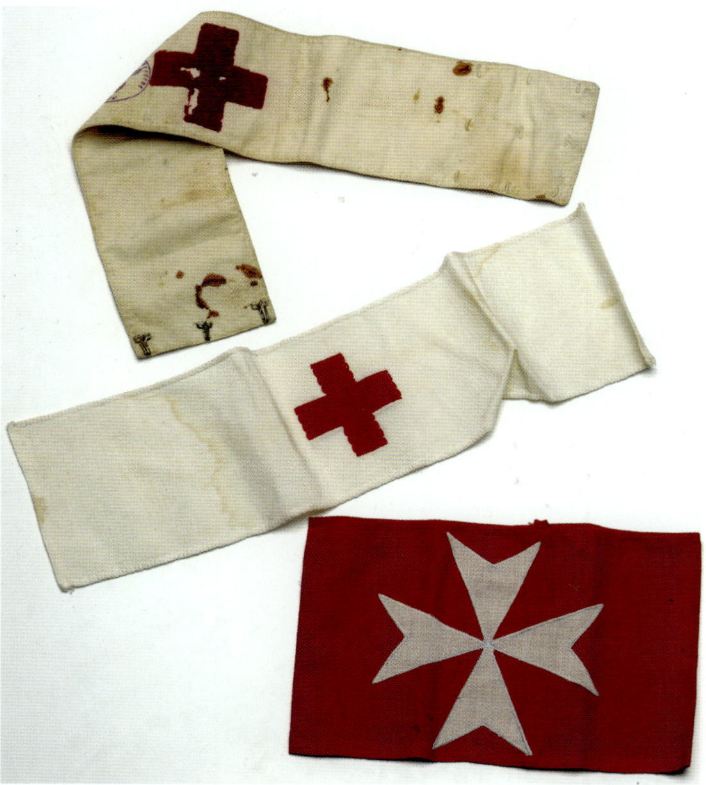

Red Cross armbands/brassards (Bulgarian: *Cherven Krust* German: *Roten Kreuze*) and Austrian Maltese Cross armband. Volunteers who belonged to the Order of the Knights of Malta wore this armband. The armband at the top shows signs of wear because it was worn by a medic who served in both World Wars as the circular ink stamp indicates.

(Bottom) (*left*) Leather field apothecary with glass medicine bottle, bandage and pair of period scissors. (*right*) Glass bottle with carrying basket for antibacterial liquid.

Forward and reverse views of various sizes and models of *Bézard* compasses. These compasses were often referred to as the Model 1910 or *Armeemodell I* and were usually privately purchased. Note the various carrying cases as well as the original box with instruction sheet. In addition, there is also a map gauge featured as well.

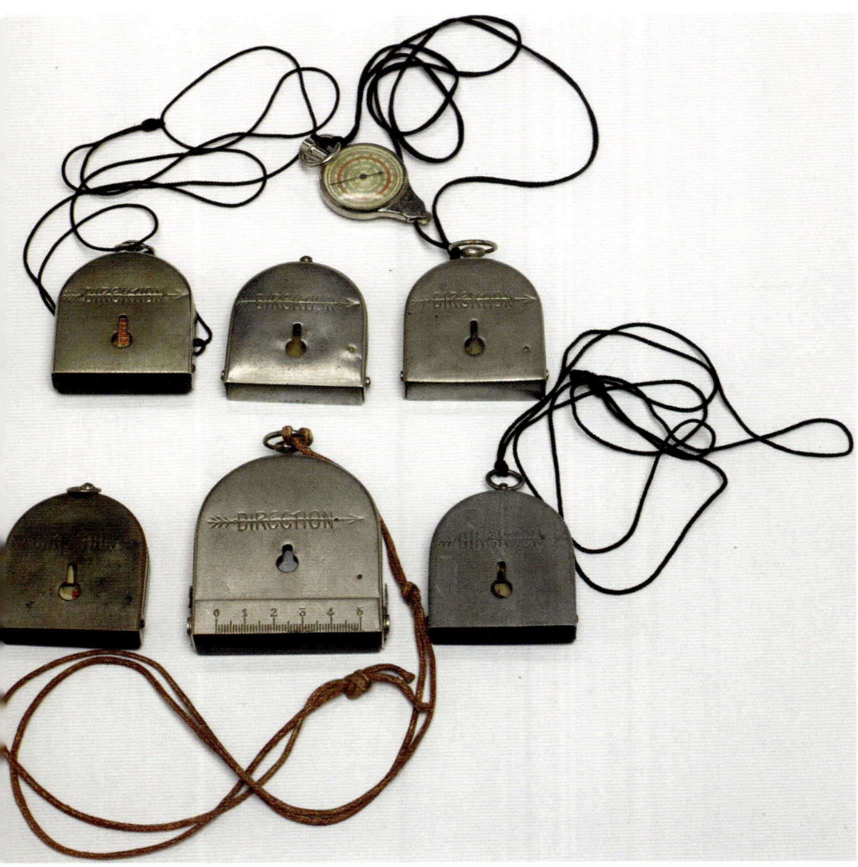

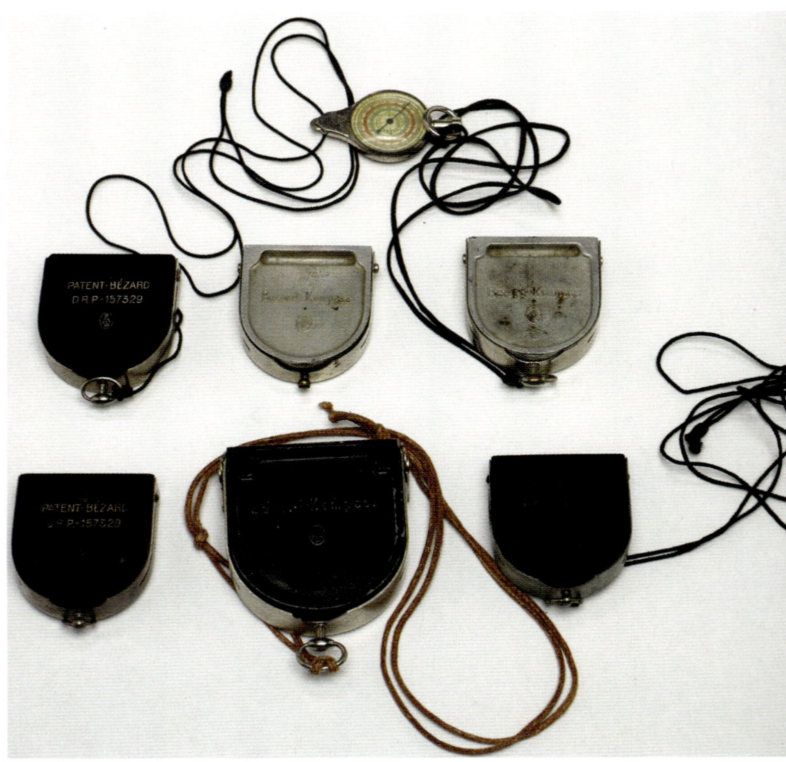

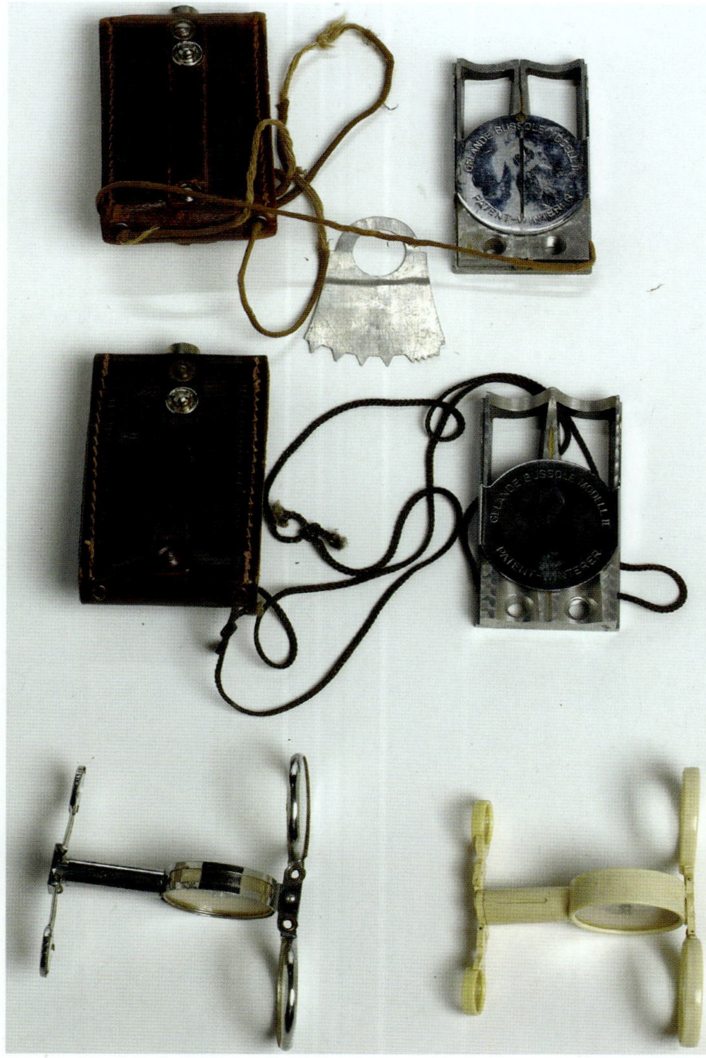

(Top) Forward and reverse views of two compasses in leather carrying cases with instruction gauge. (Bottom) Forward and reverse views of two compasses that could be used as binoculars.

Two models of binoculars (Bulgarian: *Binokal* German: *Fernglas*) and four models of leather carrying cases. Note the various markings.

Field telephone (Bulgarian: *Polevi telefon* German: *Feldtelefon*). Note the instruction manuals as well the forward and reverse views of a matching pair of gold stitched collar insignia.

Trench periscope. Note that the openings closed and the scope could be used as a weapon in hand-to-hand combat.

Metal candle lantern with wood handle and glass lenses used by the armed forces. The lenses are clear and blue. Such lanterns lighted dugouts or trench lines. Note the *DRGM* (*Deutsches Reichs Gebrauchs Muster*).

Foldable metal candle lantern. Note the *Dolomit* (Dolomite) manufacturer name.

Lantern with protective metal covers and two styles of wood carrying cases with leather and metal fittings. This model of lantern also came with a wooden shaft on the handle. The shaft could then be inserted into the barrel of a rifle while on a night watch or march. Note the depot stamp inside the wood case on the left as well as the various shades of field gray paint.

Left: Pickaxe with protective leather cover. Right: Three models of entrenching shovels and two models of leather carriers with metal fittings. Note the shovel on the far right with a serrated edge. The carrier for this shovel is featured on the right and has a protective metal insert to keep the serrated edge from cutting into the leather.

Two wood and metal boxes for *Schwarzlose* machinegun ammunition. These two boxes are compact variants and were easier to transport. Pre to early war boxes were taller.

Forward and reverse views of rare NCO (*Unteroffizier*) and officer (*Offizier*) sabers (*Säbel*) for *Landwehr* mountain troops (Gebirgstruppen). These two sabers were not shortened by the soldiers but, were made this way by the manufacturer. Shorter sabers allowed troops to maneuver better in mountainous terrain. Note the various styles of sword knots.

Detailed close-up shot of the maker mark on the blade of NCO saber for mountain troops (*Unteroffiziersäbel für Landwehrgebirgstruppen*) featured on the previous page.

Above and below: Detailed views of the saber officer saber for mountain troops (*Offiziersäbel für Landwehrgebirgstruppen*) featured on the previous page.

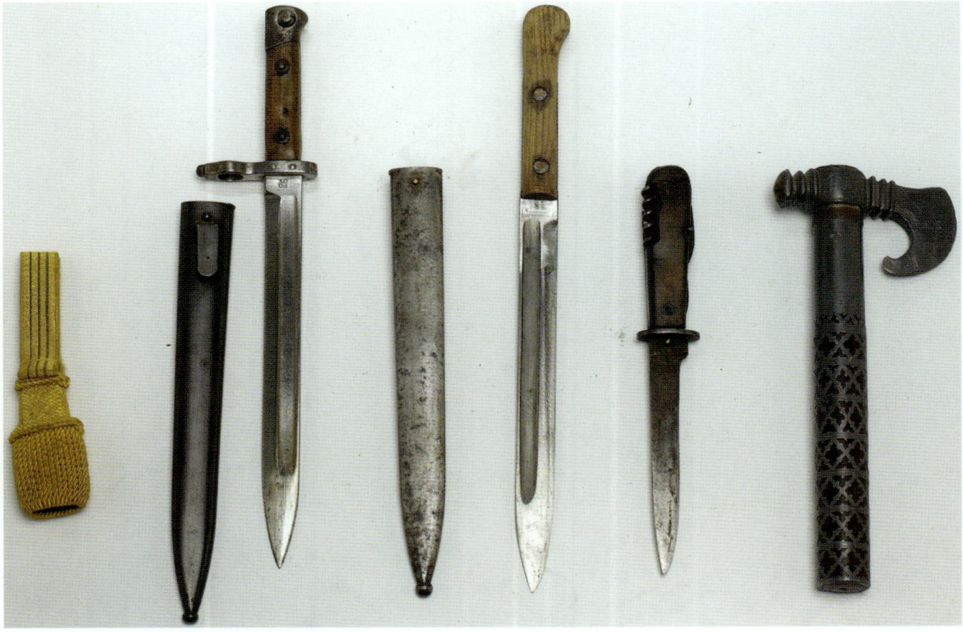

From left to right: Unused/issued Portepee bearing the letter "*K*" for Kaiser Karl, M95 bayonet , M95 bayonet with modified wood handle for use as a fighting knife, fighting knife with modified handle, and trench club with ornate lead inlay.

Detailed views of the manufacturer and regimental markings on the M95 bayonet featured on the previous page.

Detailed shots of the interior and depot stamps of two-section Model 1895 ammunition pouch (*Patronentasche*) made of brown leather with metal fittings featured on the following page. Note the stitching.

Detailed shots of the interior and depot stamps of the two rare ersatz Model 1895 ammunition pouches featured on the following page. Note the riveting (*Vernietung*).

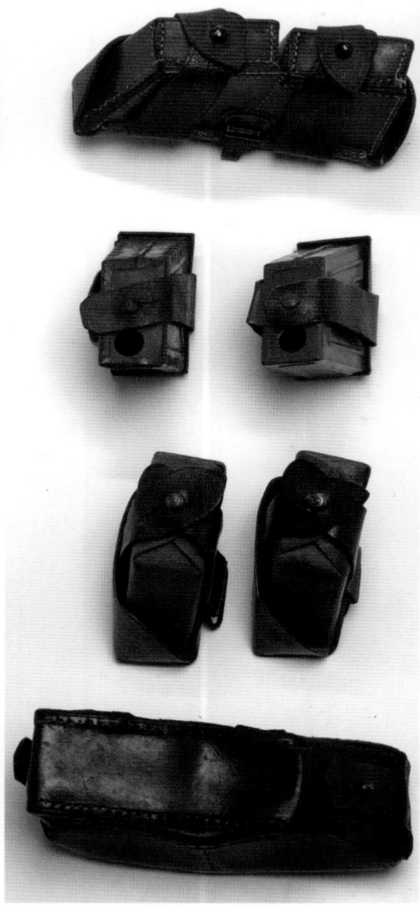

Row 1 Forward, reverse and bottom views of a two-section Model 1895 ammunition pouch (*Patronentasche*) made of brown leather with metal fittings. This model was intended for intended for the M95infantry rifle whereby single pouches were for the M95 carbine. Row 2 Forward, reverse and bottom views of Model 1895 ammunition pouches made of sheet metal painted field gray. Note the leather fasteners. Row 3 Forward, reverse and bottom views of rare ersatz Model 1895 ammunition pouches made of stiffened cardboard with leather and metal fittings. Row 4 Forward, reverse and bottom views of a Model 1888 ammunition pouch (*Patronentasche*) for the Model 1888 rifle for Austro-Hungarian infantry troops.

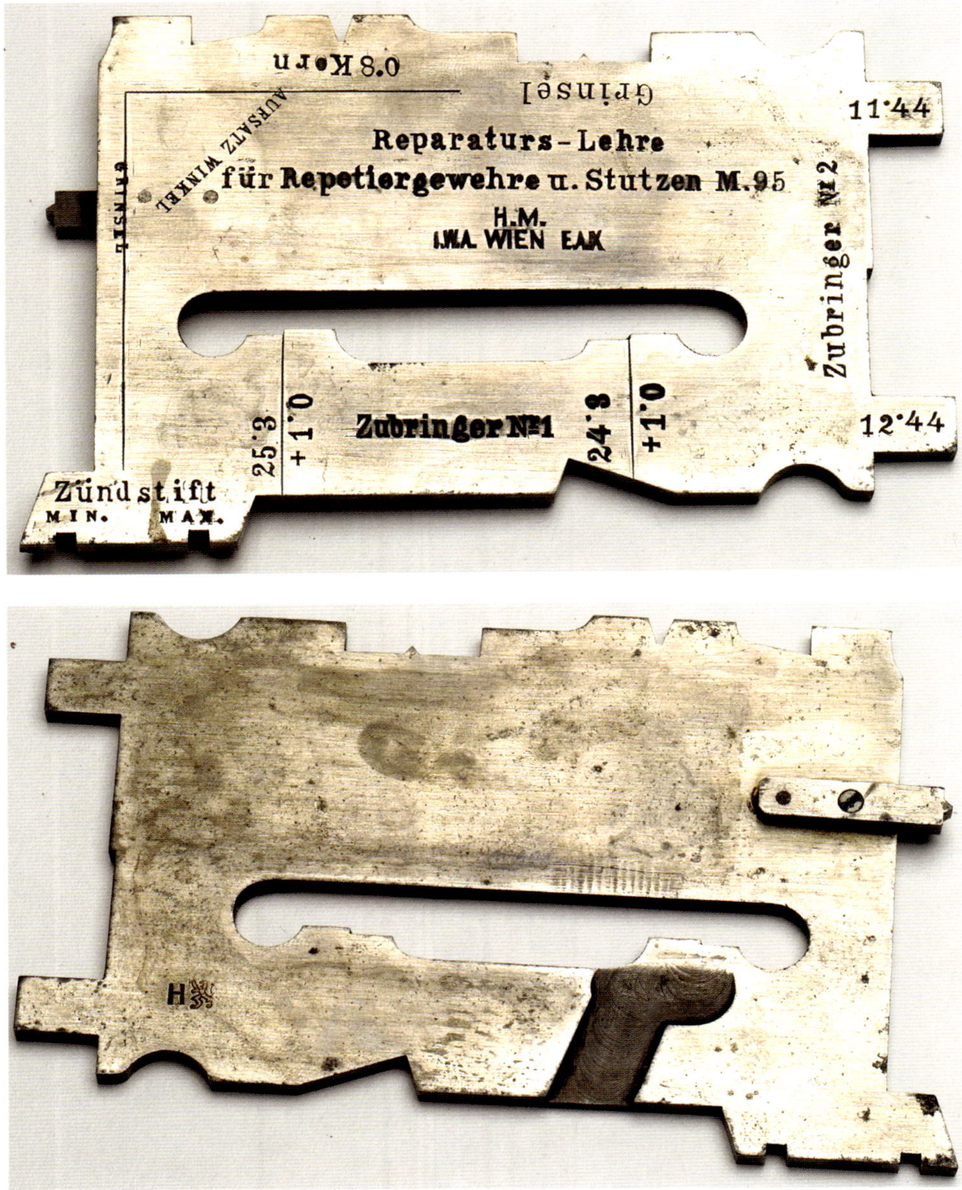

Forward and reverse views of an adjustment tool for the Model 1895 *Repetiergewehr* and *Stutzen*.

Lanyard clip

(Top) Above: Views of both sides of a Model 1895 rifle manufactured in Steyr. (Bottom) Views of both sides of a wood training rifle with metal fittings and stitched leather muzzle cover.

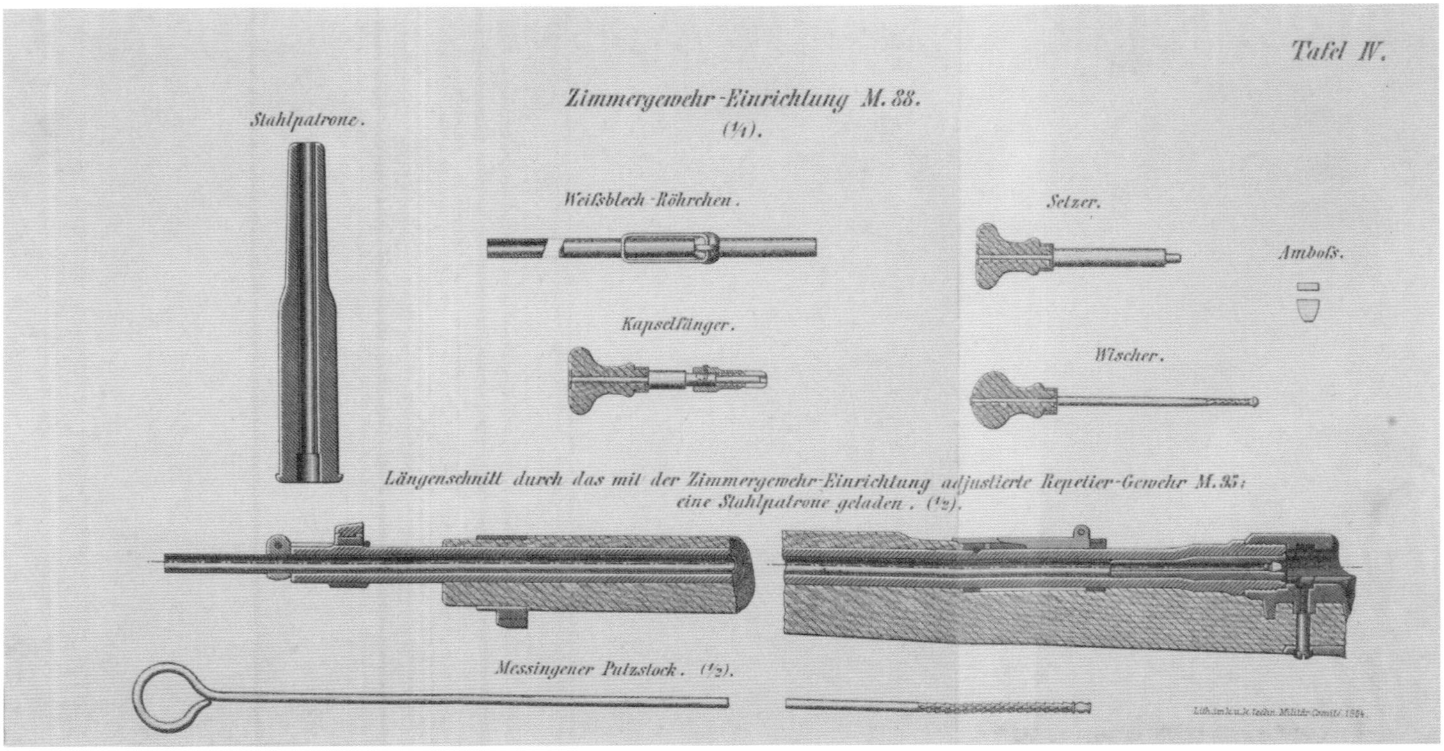
Tafel IV.
Zimmergewehr-Einrichtung M. 88.
(1/1).
Stahlpatrone.
Weißblech-Röhrchen.
Setzer.
Amboß.
Kapselfänger.
Wischer.
Längenschnitt durch das mit der Zimmergewehr-Einrichtung adjustierte Repetier-Gewehr M. 95: eine Stahlpatrone geladen. (1/2).
Messingener Putzstock. (1/2).

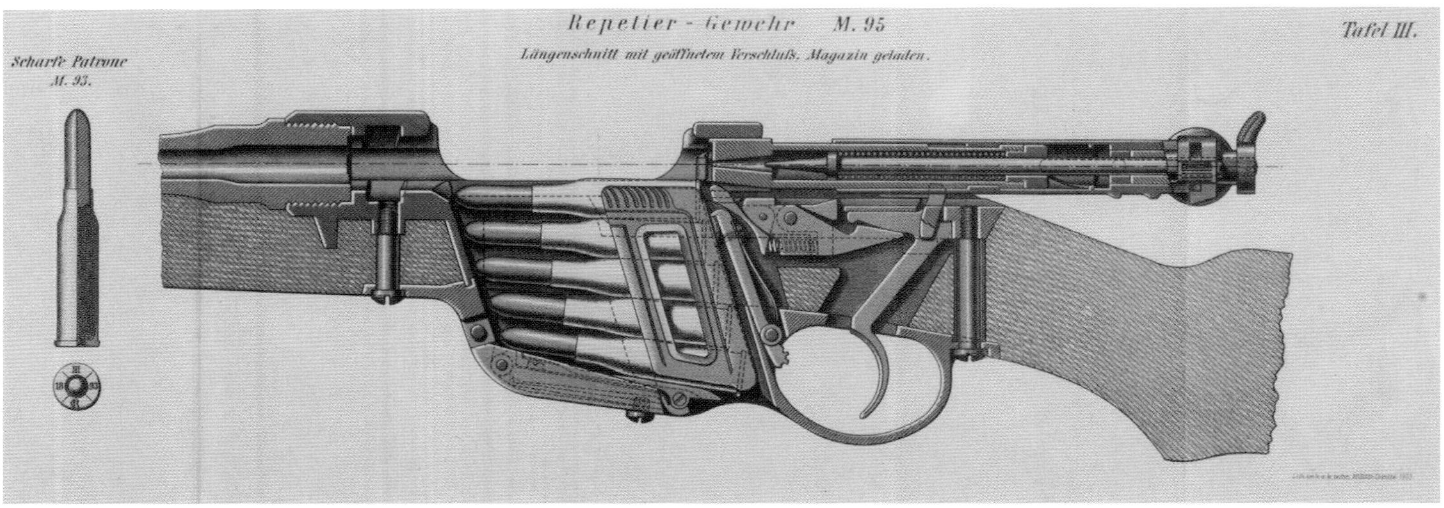
Repetier-Gewehr M. 95
Längenschnitt mit geöffnetem Verschluß, Magazin geladen.
Tafel III.
Scharfe Patrone M. 93.

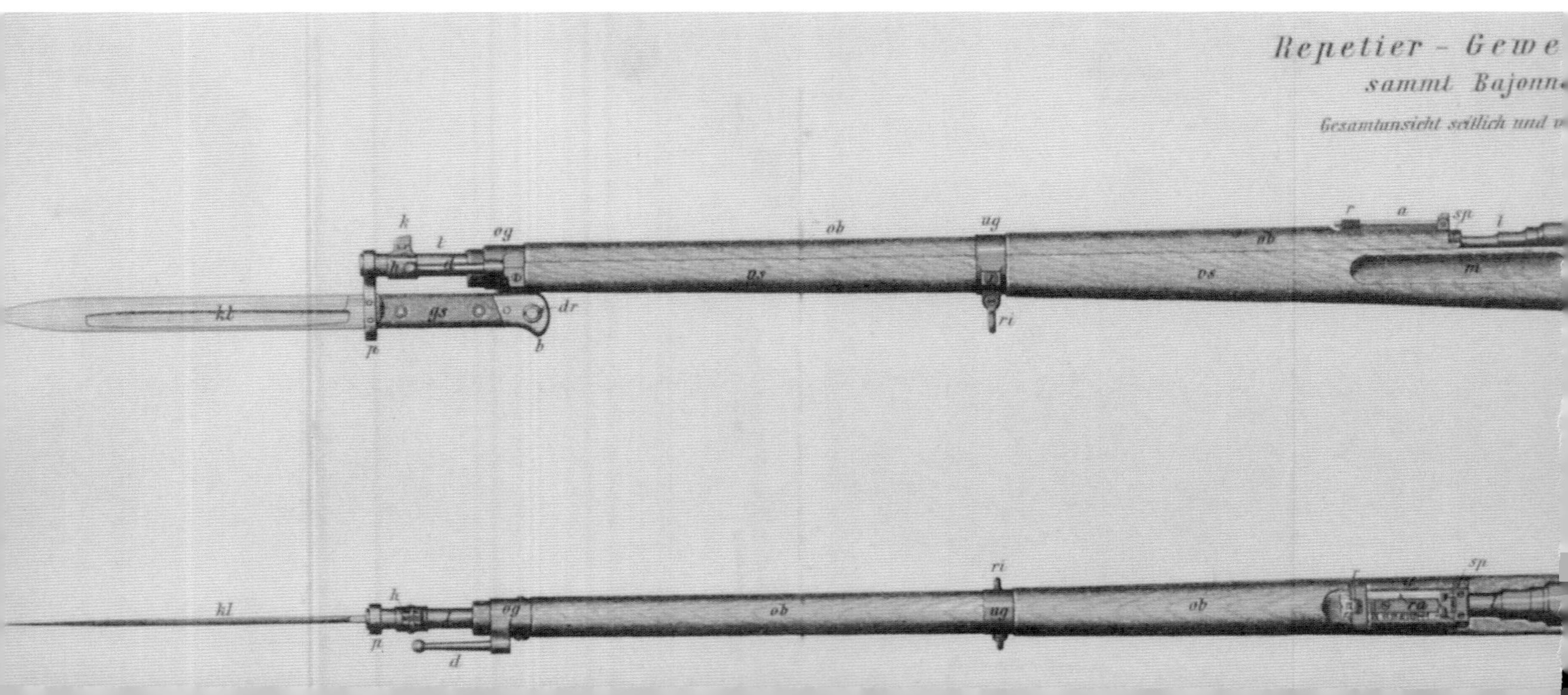
Repetier - Gewe
sammt Bajonn
Gesamtansicht seitlich und v

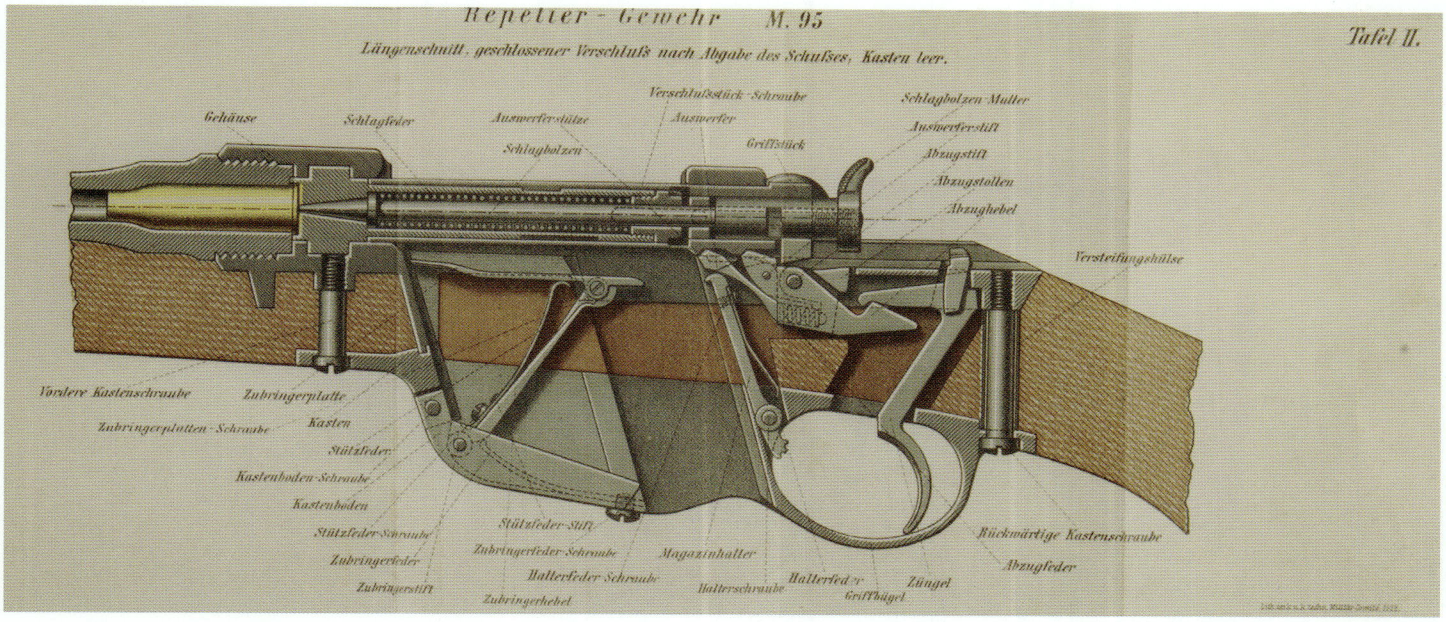

Detailed cutaway diagrams on the Model 1895 rifle.

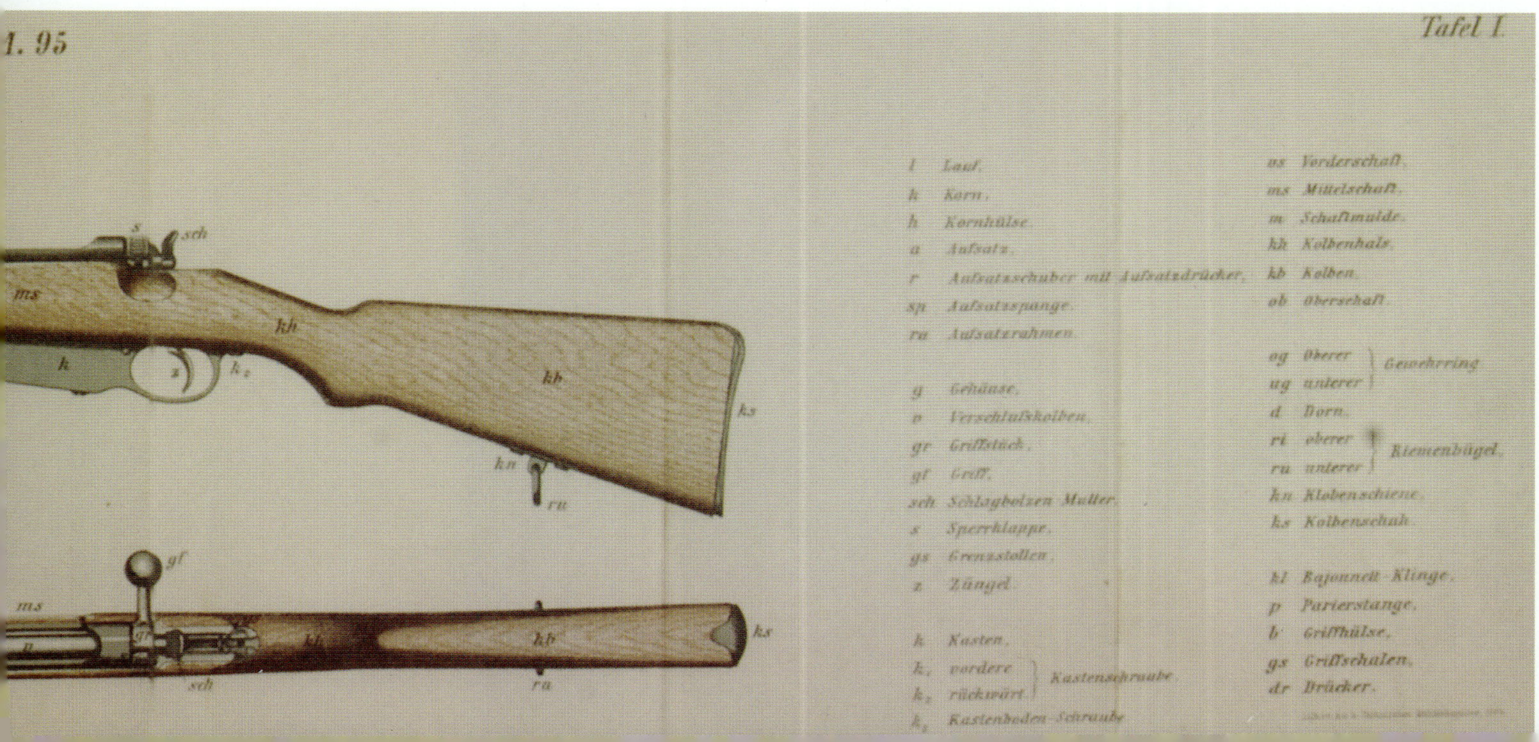

Glossary

German/Austrian/Deutsch

Abänderung: Field modification/alteration
Abflug: take-off (aviation)
Ablenkungsmänover: diversionary tactic/maneuver
Achsellrolle: padded shoulder roll
Admiralstab: Naval staff
Angriff: Attack
Artillerie: Artillery
Arzt: (m) Medical doctor
Ausrustung: Equipment
Bataillon: Battalion
Beamten: Civil servants/officials
Befehl: order (i.e. to be given an order)
Befestigung: Fortification
Bergführer: Mountain guide
Besatzung: Occupy
Bootsmann: Boatswain
Bruckenkopf: Bridgehead
Bronzene Jubiläumshofmedaille: Jubillee Medal in bronze
Bronzene Tapferkeitsmedaille: Bravery medal in bronze
Dienst: Service
Dienstgrad: Rank
Drücker: Trigger
Einkreisen: Surround
Elfenbein Griff: Ivory handle/grip. Many soldiers sought to enhance the look of their saber, bayonet or side arm by replacing the grips/handle with ivory.
Fahne: Banner
Fähnrich: Cadet (Navy/Kriegsmarine) Midshipman.
Feldzug: Campaign
Feuer einstellen: Cease fire
Feind/ fiendlich: Enemy
Festung: Fortress
Flotte: Fleet
Gegenangriff: Counter attack
Gegner: Enemy
Geleit: Convoy
Generalstab: General staff
Gepanzert: Armored
Granatsplitter: Shell splinter/sharpnel
Gruppe: Team/Squad
Kamerad: Comrade
Kameraden: Comrades (plural)
Korn: Frontal sight on a firearm.

Bulgarian/Bulgarski

Artileriiski: Artillery
Artileriiski Snarjad: Artillery shell/round
Bashlak: Hood/Cowl. Similar to a Czarist Russian *bashlik*.
Bejantzi: Refugees
Binokal: Binoculars
Bombi: Grenade/Bomb
Botushi: Boots
Bushlat: Navy P-Coat
Cherven Krust: Red Cross
Divisiya: Division
Efreytor: Corporal
Emblema: Badge/Emblem
Feldfebel: First Sergeant
Flota: Navy
Granati: Grenade
Granatomat: Grenade launcher / Granatenwerfer
Gueneral: General
Hulmove: Hills
Kalpak: Fur cap
Kandidat Podoficer: Non-commissioned officer (NCO)
Kapitan: Captain
Kartechnitza: Machinegun
Karzarma: Barracks/Caserne
Kaska: Steel Helmet /Stahlhelm
Kavaleria: Cavalry
Keppe: Field Cap
Keppeta: Field caps (plural)
Kobur: Holster
Kolan: Belt
Kokarda: Cockade
Lopata: Shovel
Mayor: Major
Medal: Medal
Moriak: Sailor
Minohvargachka: Grenade launcher / Minenwerfer
Naves: Tents
Ofitzer: Officer
Okop: Trench
Okupatziya: Occupation
Opanci: A style of Balkan footwear
Orden: Order
Orden Kiril I Metodij: Order of Saint Cyril and Methodius. This Order was established by Czar Ferdinand I in 1909.
Orudie: Field cannon
Palto: Overcoat/Greatcoat
Pantaloni: Pants
Patrondash: Ammunition pouch
Pistolet: Pistol
Planina: Mountains
Polevi telefon: Field telephone
Polk: Regiment
Polkovnik: Colonel
Podporuchik: Second Lieutenant
Poruchik: First Lieutenant
Protivogas: Gasmask
Protivovazdushna: Anti-aircraft
Pushka: Rifle
Ranistza: Rucksack
Ranen: Wounded
Rednik: Private
Remak: Shoulder boards

Revolver: Revolver
Rotmeister: Cavalry Captain
Sabja: Saber
Sanitaren: Medic
Sestra: Nurse
Sestri: Nurses
Shinel: Overcoat/Greatcoat
Shtik: Bayonet
Shturmovi Voyski: Assault/Storm troops *Sturmtruppen*
Skala: Tunic
Starshi: Sergeant
Svarzochni voiski: Signal troops
Sveshtennick: Regimental Priest
Tropicheski Shlem: Tropical/ Sun helmet
Tzarvuli: A traditional style of footwear native to the Balkans
Ubit: Killed
Vazdushni Sili: Air force
Voenen: Military
Voenen Orkestar: Military Orchestra/Band
Voenni Obuvki: Field shoes
Voin: Warrior
Voinik: Soldier
Voinitzi: Soldiers (plural)
Zemlyanka: Bunker/Dugout
Znacka: Badge

Hungarian/ Magyar

Ágyu: Field Cannon
Aknavetö: Grenade launcher / Minenwerfer
Alezredes: Lieutenant Colonel
Altiszt: Non-commissioned officer (NCO)
Becanscok: Field shoes / laced ankle boots\
Börlábszáróvók: Leather legging /gaiters
Csákó: Shako
Császár é kiralyi: Imperial and royal (*k.u.k.*)
Csendör: Military Police/Gendarme
Dolmány: Tunic
Diszruhát: Uniform
Galler: Collar
Hajtóka: Collar patch (*paroli*)
Ing: Shirt
Jelvény: Badge
Kard: Sword /saber
Kardbojt: sword knot
Keztyük: Gloves
Köpeny: Overcoat/Greatcoat
Lábszáróvók: Puttees /leggings
Mente: This refers to a style of coat known as an "Attila" with a fur collar.
Nyakravaló: A collar guard/protector used to keep the wool from rubbing against a soldier's neck.
Pisztolytáska: Holster
Ruházat: Outfitting
Szurony: Bayonet
Szuronytáska: Bayonet frog/holder
Tekercscsel: padded shoulder roll
Tizedes: Corporal
Töltény: Ammunition
Tölténytáska: Ammunition pouch
Tüzér: Artillerist (Cannonier)
Üteg: Batterie
Vár: Fortress
Vezérkár: General Staff
Vonat: Train
Zászlóalj: Battalion

Ukrainian Ukra*yi*ns'kyy

Artyl*e*riya: Artillery
Bahn*e*t: Bayonet
Batal'y*o*n: Battalion
Biy/B*y*tva: Battle
Cherev*y*ky: Boots
Harm*a*ta: Cannon
Hran*a*ta: Grenade
Kan*a*va: Trench
Kaval*e*riya: Cavalry
Khor*o*brist'/ Smilyvist': Bravery
Kobur*a*: Holster
Kok*a*rda: Cockade
Lehion*e*r: Legionnaire
Patr*o*ny: Ammunition
Pikh*o*ta: Infantry
Rushn*y*tsia: Rifle
S*u*mka: Haversack
Tunika: Tunic
Viys'k*o*v*y*y: Military
Vzvod: Platoon

Further Reading

Uniforms and Equipment of the Austro-Hungarian Army in World War One, Spencer A. Coil, Schiffer Publishing Ltd., Atglen PA, 2003

Uniforms and Equipment of the Czarist Russian Armed Forces in World War I, Spencer Anthony Coil, Schiffer Publishing Ltd., Atglen PA, 2005

Uniforms and Equipment of the French Armed Forces in World War I, Spencer Anthony Coil, Schiffer Publishing Ltd., Atglen PA, 2005

Uniforms and Equipment of the Italian Armed Forces in World War I, Dr. Spencer Anthony Coil, Schiffer Publishing Ltd., Atglen PA, 2006

The Balkan War 1912-1913, Alexander Vachkov, Angela Publishing, Bulgaria.

Le Armi e gli Equipaggiamenti dell'esceritoAustro –Ungarico dal 1914 al 1918. Uniformi-Distintivi-Buffetterie. Volume primo., Siro Offelli, Gino Rossato Editore. Via bella Venezia. 2001.

L'Artiglieria Austo-Ungaricnella Grande Guerra. Filippo Cappelano.Gino Rossato Editore. Via bella Venezia. 2001.

Királyért é Hazáért Barcy Zoltán. Somogyi Gyõzõ Corvina. Hungary 1990.